Politics as a Christian Vocation

Many democratic citizens, including many Christians, think that separation of religion from the state means the exclusion of religious beliefs from the political process. That view is mistaken. Both democracy and Christian faith, this book shows, call all Christians to make their beliefs effective in politics. But the discussion here differs from others. Most have trouble relating religion to democratic discussion and debate because they assume that religious differences cannot be publicly debated. Against this majority view, this book argues that Christian faith belongs in politics because it shares with democracy full commitment to the way of reason. The book then develops ideals of justice and the common good Christians should advocate within the democratic process and shows the difference these ideals make for contemporary politics in the United States, focusing specifically on issues of abortion, affirmative action, and economic distribution.

Franklin I. Gamwell is Shailer Mathews Professor of Religious Ethics, Theology, and Philosophy of Religions at The Divinity School, The University of Chicago, where he has taught since 1979. He is the author of four books, including most recently *Democracy on Purpose: Justice and the Reality of God* (2000).

Politics as a Christian Vocation

Faith and Democracy Today

FRANKLIN I. GAMWELL

University of Chicago

CAMBRIDGE
UNIVERSITY PRESS

PUBLISHED BY THE PRESS SYNDICATE OF THE UNIVERSITY OF CAMBRIDGE
The Pitt Building, Trumpington Street, Cambridge, United Kingdom

CAMBRIDGE UNIVERSITY PRESS
The Edinburgh Building, Cambridge CB2 2RU, UK
40 West 20th Street, New York, NY 10011-4211, USA
477 Williamstown Road, Port Melbourne, VIC 3207, Australia
Ruiz de Alarcón 13, 28014 Madrid, Spain
Dock House, The Waterfront, Cape Town 8001, South Africa

http://www.cambridge.org

First published 2005

Printed in the United States of America

Typeface Palatino 10/13.5 pt. *System* LaTeX 2_ε [TB]

A catalog record for this book is available from the British Library.

Library of Congress Cataloging in Publication Data
Gamwell, Franklin I.
Politics as a Christian vocation : faith and democracy today /
Franklin I. Gamwell.
p. cm.
Includes bibliographical references and index.
ISBN 0-521-83876-2 – ISBN 0-521-54752-0 (pbk.)
1. Christianity and politics. 2. Democracy – Religious aspects –
Christianity. 3. Christianity and justice. I. Title.

BR115.P7G315 2004
261.7–dc22 2004045101

ISBN 0 521 83876 2 hardback
ISBN 0 521 54752 0 paperback

To
William Sloane Coffin

Contents

Contents

Preface

This work owes a substantial debt to Protestants for the Common Good, a Chicago-based organization of clergy and laity who seek better to articulate and pursue politics as a Christian vocation. Begun in 1995 in response to perceived injustices in our contemporary public life and the perceived failures of Protestant Christianity to address them adequately, this group has offered me the occasion to reflect on the relation of Christian faith and democracy today. More importantly, the venture has provided a company of Christians whose practical wisdom and commitment to justice have advanced my education. Without the benefit received from their deliberations, including their critical consideration of some things said here, this work would be much the worse. Nothing said here speaks for that organization or any other member of it, and some of my friends there will find ample room for disagreement. But I am deeply grateful for the community Protestants for the Common Good has given me.

I am also indebted to academic colleagues and friends who favored my requests for their help and were generous with their critical proposals for revision: Philip E. Devenish, Larry L. Greenfield, Margaret M. Mitchell, Schubert M. Ogden, and Alexander I. Vishio. In addition, extensive reviews and suggestions were offered by three anonymous readers for Cambridge University Press, all of whom have significantly altered the work. Naturally, none of these people is responsible for the deficiencies in my discussion, and each may think that I have not taken due notice of some comments she or he made. On my accounting, nonetheless, each has improved the work, and to each I express my thanks. I am further grateful to Alex Vishio for his thoughtful preparation of the index.

This work includes in revised form some paragraphs from papers I have previously published. I have drawn, in Chapter 2, from my essay "Democracy and the Theological Task," *The Journal of Religion* 82 (July 2002): 349–64; in Chapter 5, from my essay "Politics as a Religious Question," in *Belonging Together: Faith and Politics in a Relational World*, edited by Douglas Sturm, Claremont, CA: P&F Press, 2003, pp. 31–43; and, in Chapter 6, from my article "Affirmative Action: Is It Democratic?" *The Christian Century* (January 24, 1996): 77–80. I am grateful for permission to use this material.

I take the liberty of dedicating the book to the Reverend William Sloane Coffin, whose witness to the Christian faith has been, far beyond his knowing, profoundly important to me throughout my adult life. I do not imply that he agrees with all I have said, much less that my discussion does justice to his exemplary practice of politics as a Christian vocation. I intend only to express my abiding gratitude and admiration.

Politics as a Christian Vocation

Introduction

The Present Purpose

United States politics has always been challenged by its relation to religion, because the First Amendment endorses religious freedom and thus religious plurality. During the past fifty years, this relation has become especially controversial because of increasing diversity among the nation's religions and the increasing consequence of government in our lives. In both larger public and specifically academic discussion and debate, views on the role religious convictions and arguments should or should not play in our common life range from the privatization of religion to its indispensable role in the pursuit of justice. Often, disagreements occur in the context of debate over specific political issues – for instance, the permissibility of abortion, the legitimacy and importance of affirmative action, the due forms of criminal justice, the fair distribution of wealth and income, the required treatment of our natural habitat, and the moral propriety of some given military engagement.

But if our politics must determine its relation to religious plurality, so, correspondingly, does any given religious community face the question of its relation to politics. This work pursues how Christians should ask and answer the latter question. I seek to clarify whether and, if so, how active participation in contemporary politics is a Christian calling. Politically, the discussion is focused principally on the American republic. But that focus itself requires address to general questions about the life of Christian witness. Clearly, the responsibilities of Christians in our setting cannot be clarified without asking about the meaning or content of Christian faith and what, if any, abiding relation to political community it prescribes. The answers given in this work to such general questions have, I believe, considerably wider importance. Still, my intent is to speak about Christian commitment today within the United States, and more basic understandings are pursued for the sake of relevance to it. Focused in this way, then, the book is about contemporary politics as a Christian vocation.

The idea of "vocation," which means a calling or a summons, has a long history within the Christian community. In medieval thought, the term was typically reserved for a divine calling to specifically religious activities, especially to the priesthood or the monastic life, and bore hierarchical connotations. Having a vocation in this sense was being authorized for a higher form of service to God. Following the Reformation, "vocation" was released from its restricted usage and, correspondingly, from its hierarchical connotations. Summarily speaking, it came to mean, at least for Protestants, a calling to some distinct occupation or set of responsibilities as an occasion for witness to God's presence and redeeming activity. Thus, any honest and useful work could be a Christian vocation. The difference between specifically religious and other callings important to human life and the human community became solely one of function, with no sense of higher and lower, so that, for instance, being a member of the clergy and being a farmer could not be ranked in terms of service to God (see Dillenberger and Welch: 49, 234–5). All Christians, we might say, were equally called to be Christians, and the differing vocations given to differing Christians were equally important forms of that more fundamental identity.

Subsequently, "vocation" also acquired a secular meaning, in distinction from designating a Christian calling to some kind of secular activity, and the term now sometimes signifies simply any occupation or business or profession. But there is, even in this secular usage, a legacy from the earlier religious import, because taking one's work as a vocation often means that one is called to this kind of activity as a contribution to the common good. Whether one works as a farmer or teacher or artist or craftsman, one does so vocationally when one not only strives for success in that particular enterprise but also understands it in view of its importance to the larger context of our life together. In this sense, one might speak of differing kinds of activity as specifications of the moral vocation given to us all. Accordingly, the secular idea of a specific vocation can be extended from application to one's principal work or central set of activities and used to designate any specific practice it may be morally useful or important to distinguish from others. Thus, one can speak of one's vocation to be a parent or citizen or friend.

Returning to the Christian context, we may also consider vocations that specify the Christian commitment and do not necessarily mark a form of work central to a person's life. They are distinguished simply because doing so is important to the inclusive purpose of the church. Some of these vocations may be given to Christians generally, whatever occupation or ministry may distinguish one Christian from another. In this sense, they can be called common Christian vocations. For instance, we might discuss being compassionate, the practice of serving those afflicted or grieving, as a specific activity to which Christians generally are called, even if they are not commonly called to receive specialized training in pastoral care or counseling. Similarly, we might speak of care for children, encouraging and educating their growth and integrity, as a common Christian vocation, even if some Christians will properly attend more fully than others to this task. Or, again, perhaps theology is a vocation of Christians generally, meaning that all are called to reflect for themselves, insofar as they are able, on the meaning and truth of their faith when these become problematic, even if only some Christians have the specialized vocation of being a professional theologian.

A common Christian vocation, then, is a Christian calling that does not distinguish some Christians from others by commission to specialized responsibilities within the Christian community or to a certain kind of secular work as one's principal occupation. In this sense, the present work asks about politics as a common Christian vocation. Hence, the discussion is not focused on politics as a specialized profession, whereby a Christian might seek or hold political office or in some other way choose participation in the formal political process as her or his principal work. To the contrary, our concern is how Christian faith relates to membership in the political community. Given that all Christians are citizens, does their calling to a life of faith include a common calling to political activity and, if so, toward what ends? In this formulation, "political activity" means the deliberate attempt to influence or help shape political rule and, thereby, to determine the consequences of political order for all affected by it. If, for some or all Christians, the life of faith does not include a political vocation, we can still say that their faith implies something about their political responsibilities, namely, that they should be or may be politically quiescent.

In the United States and the wider contemporary world, many Christians believe that political participation is an obvious and, indeed, central part of the Christian calling itself. Hence, they may counsel, asking *whether* Christians have such responsibilities is hardly necessary. In fact, however, those so persuaded depart from a profound tradition in Christian thought, for which the life of common Christian witness does not include political activity. As I will discuss, this view stretches back to early Christian self-understanding, and, in the expression given there, I will call it the "early account" of Christian political responsibility. Its effect in subsequent Christian life and thought, right up to the present, has been considerable. I, too, will argue for an understanding contrary to that tradition. But seeing why the early account excluded politics from the common witness of Christians and why Christians today should reach a different conclusion is, I will try to show, important for explicating the political ends contemporary Christians should pursue.

This is because a clarified departure from that tradition requires attention to modern political communities that are or approach being democratic. I will argue that politics today is a common Christian vocation because the moral principles implied by Christian faith prescribe, at least in our setting, democracy as a form of political rule and thus democratic citizenship as a general form of Christian witness. As I will try to show in due course, however, this interpretation of Christian belief is controversial because the presuppositions of modern democratic politics, including especially the constitutional provision for religious freedom, are at odds with some basic understandings of their faith pervasively shared by Christians past and present. One prominent case in point concerns what Christians mean or think they mean in claiming truth for their convictions about God and human life. Democracy, I will argue, can only be politics through full and free political discussion and debate or politics by the way of reason; only those political claims that can be validated in reasoned discourse should direct the decisions or activities of the state. In contrast, the majority voice in the Christian tradition has denied that the truth of Christian belief can be fully redeemed without appeal to God's special self-disclosure through Jesus Christ. Christian commitment to democracy also implies, in other words, a departure from this majority voice.

In sum, asking whether politics is a common Christian vocation will provide the context in which to spell out the nature of democracy, formulate its challenge, and reconsider the meaning of Christian faith. Proceeding in this way will prove useful because showing why Christian belief prescribes government by the way of reason is incomplete without explicating Christian conceptions of justice and the common good. I will argue that Christians generally are called to democratic activity because they are called to pursue the community of love and to act for justice as general emancipation. While confirming that politics is a common Christian vocation, then, the argument will also define the ends for which Christians should choose their political purposes.

Chapter 1 will review summarily the relation of Christian faith to politics as articulated during the early Christian movement in order to ask whether its exclusion of political activity from the prescribed witness of Christians generally should be accepted today. Chapter 2 will discuss the emergence of modern democracy, the character of a democratic political community, and its challenge to some inherited understandings of Christian faith. Chapters 3 and 4 will respond to this challenge by showing that Christian faith prescribes the way of reason and defines democratic principles of justice.

Chapters 5 and 6 will illustrate the importance of these principles to contemporary politics in the United States. Chapter 5 will discuss religious decisions at stake in public life today, in the sense that disagreements about particular political issues reflect the influence, however tacit, of conflicting ideals for the human community. This discussion centers on religious differences reflected in disputes about domestic political purposes. I believe that a similar and, in significant measure, overlapping analysis can be given with respect to issues concerning this country's relation to the larger world that have become prominent in the early twenty-first century. Seeking to provide that analysis would, however, substantially and unnecessarily complicate the treatment. My intent is to illustrate how politics implicates religious decisions and, thereby, to suggest how the political witness of Christians makes a difference of some moment in our contemporary public life. Chapter 6, then, will further illustrate the significance of these religious choices through comment on three specific political issues: abortion, affirmative action, and economic distribution.

Chapter 1

Render to Caesar

Christians who ask about their political responsibility often find themselves bound somehow to make sense of the New Testament dictum "Render to Caesar the things that are Caesar's, and to God the things that are God's" (Mark 12:17; cf. Matthew 22:21). In the Gospel of Mark, Jesus gave this response when asked whether Jews were obligated to pay the taxes levied by their Roman rulers, and the dictum is relevant to our question if we take "Caesar" to symbolize political rule in general and the payment or withholding of taxes, each in its own way, to symbolize proper response to the rulers. The answer Jesus gave may then seem relevant to how contemporary Christians should understand their relation to politics.

It is probable that Roman taxes were deeply resented by many Jewish people, much as American colonists in the eighteenth century were offended by taxes levied by Parliament. In Mark's story, the question was put to Jesus by certain Pharisees and Herodians who sought to trap him. If he replied in the affirmative, the Jewish people generally would think him a traitor; if in the negative, he would suffer the disfavor and suspicion of the Roman rulers. His cryptic response served to confound the inquisitors, since Jesus did not specify which things belong to Caesar and which to God. Henry David Thoreau said that Jesus left his inquisitors "no wiser than before as to which was which, for they did not wish to know" (cited in Buttrick: 519). But this means that Jesus did not state whether payment is required. At least to first appearances, it is uncertain what, if anything, contemporary Christians might learn from this dictum about their political responsibilities.

Indeed, the story can be the more perplexing because Jesus seems to imply that some things are properly given to Caesar in distinction from God. In contrast, nothing seems more persistent throughout the New Testament than this: The One whom Jesus reveals is the abiding source and end of all things, without whose all-embracing power none could exist and in whose all-embracing love each and all have their only ultimate meaning or significance – and, in this sense, all things belong to God. Thus, the life of Christian faith is nowhere more clearly summarized than in Mark's report of how Jesus replied to another question: "'Which commandment is the first of all?' Jesus answered, 'The first is, "Hear, O Israel: The Lord our God, the Lord is one; you shall love the Lord your God will all your heart, and with all your soul, and with all your mind, and with all your strength." The second is this, "You shall love your neighbor as yourself." There is no other commandment greater than these'" (Mark 12:28–31; cf. Matthew 22:36–9). This twofold calling is the Great Commandment because finally it is the only commandment, in the sense that all others are applications or articulations of it. We are called to love God in all that we do and, therefore, to lead our lives with no other purpose than to love all those whom God loves, and this means to treat all as individuals who belong to God. As Aquinas later wrote: "The precept of charity contains the injunction that God should be loved from our whole heart, which means that all things would be referred to God. Consequently, man cannot fulfill the precept of charity unless he also refer all things to God" (S.T. 2–1.100.10 ad 2).[1] How, then, could one who renders to God what belongs to God treat anything as if it belongs instead to Caesar?

But perhaps Mark's witness intends precisely that Jesus's directive about Caesar and God should be, as it were, read through the Great Commandment. The dictum need not be perplexing to those who confess Jesus Christ because they know that, in truth, everything belongs to God. Read in this way, the dictum means this: Just as we should love our neighbors because thereby we love God with all our heart

---

1. References to Aquinas's *Summa Theologicae* (S.T.) will designate in order the part of that summa, the number of the question, and the number of the article; when the cited material is from a response Aquinas gives to one of the objections he considers, the response will be indicated by "ad" and the number of the objection in question. Thus, the present reference is to the *Summa Theologicae*, the first part of the second part, the hundredth question, the tenth article, and the response to the second objection. The translations I have used are noted in Works Cited.

and soul and mind and strength, so we should give to Caesar whatever we need to give in order to refer all things to God. Accordingly, the question Christians should ask is not "What belongs to Caesar and what belongs to God?" but, rather, "How should someone who seeks always to serve the divine purpose relate to the political order?"

I THE EARLY ACCOUNT

In so restating the question, we follow the practice of most early thinkers, who sought to bring "the political order within the divine economy" (Wolin: 98). Writing to the church in Rome, Paul asserts that political powers are divinely ordained and thus should be accepted and obeyed. "Let every person be subject to the governing authorities; for there is no authority except from God, and those authorities that exist have been instituted by God. Therefore whoever resists authority resists what God has appointed, and those who resist will incur judgment" (Romans 13: 1–2). What prompted Paul to address this matter in this letter is open to debate. Since his exhortation is framed by explications of the love commandment, especially as it should be exemplified within "the one body in Christ" (Romans 12: 5), perhaps he was speaking to contention among Christians regarding their relation to the realm of politics, disagreement the more likely to arise in Rome.[2] Perhaps, further, his attention focused specifically on a dispute about the paying of taxes, which are mentioned explicitly a few verses later (Romans 13: 6–7), and thus one should not assume that Paul here offers a general prescription for the relation of Christians to political authority. Still, it is noteworthy that the early verses of Romans 13 contain Paul's only clear statement about political responsibility. That he did not otherwise address the subject at least suggests that active attention to the justice or injustice of the social order did not, on his view, belong to the distinctive task of Christians within the divine plan.

The larger corpus of Paul's letters more or less clearly conveys a conviction that this task centers on the character and extension of

---

2. In my discussion of Paul, I am indebted to Victor Furnish, "Uncommon Love and the Common Good: Christians as Citizens in the Letters of Paul" (see Furnish) and correspondence with its author, and also to conversations with Margaret M. Mitchell, although one or both of these scholars may still disagree with my formulations.

their own community, in which the new life of Christian faith found social expression. In 1 Thessalonians, Paul's earliest surviving letter, the principal "context for moral concern is the Christian community" (Meeks: 130), and this focus persists throughout his available writings. This is not to say that Paul permitted moral indifference toward or withdrawal from the larger society. There is ample evidence that he takes "you shall love your neighbor as yourself" to command love of all people, and this is apparent beginning with 1 Thessalonians: "See that none of you repays evil for evil; but always seek to do good to one another and to all" (1 Thessalonians 5: 15). Christians are called to be peaceful and honorable members of the wider community, to seek the good of all, precisely because God's love embraces all. Still, the Christian community is the locus of God's new creation, begun in Christ, and cultivation of the new life within this alternative community remains the principal object of Paul's moral exhortation. This focus, together with the absence of explicit political counsel other than Romans 13, at least suggests that, for Paul, larger social institutions and political rule may or should, as a general rule, be accepted because God provides through them the civilized order in which the Christian community can pursue its distinctive task. In this respect, the early verses of Romans 13 likely express Paul's more general view of political rule, so that he at least permits and, perhaps, exhorts Christians to be politically accommodating.

Moral focus on the church was, Wayne Meeks argues, widespread in the early Christian movement and helps to explain why it expressed an unusual concern for unity among the fragments dispersed within Palestine and the larger Greco-Roman world. Although conflicts "not only of opinion but of the very shape of the movement" were present "from the earliest times," they themselves betray that the church was marked by "some internal drive toward unity and even uniformity of belief and behavior" (Meeks: 120). On the reading of Sheldon Wolin, the Christian community as a new order of human relationships was a social development of immense importance. Within the legacy of Greek political understanding, still effective in the Greco-Roman world, "political membership was treated as an overriding necessity" for the good or fully human life. But the Christian, Wolin continues, "could entertain meaningful doubts about political . . . membership, because his response was not governed by a hard choice between membership in a political society and membership in no society at all" (Wolin: 102). To the contrary, the new society was "one of far greater purity and higher purpose" (Wolin: 99) and thus issued a challenge to political society with profound long-term consequences for Western politics.

Whether or not Wolin is correct about those consequences, the contrast he draws is appropriate to Paul in the following sense: Peaceful and honorable acceptance of the surrounding social order was required by the profound sense of difference that characterized and focused the early Christian community. Unlike Paul, moreover, other early Christians expressed that difference as alienation or estrangement from and, in this sense, complete rejection of the governing authorities. In the book of Revelation, for instance, condemnation of the Roman Empire is unmitigated. Still, that book "is no call for revolutionary action, but for passive resistance, for disengagement and quietism" (Meeks: 146). Hence, whether Roman rule was accommodated as God's institution or renounced as a realm thoroughly defiant of God's will, agreement seems to have been pervasive in this respect: The divine purpose directs Christians' principal attention to their common life within the new community.

This reading does not gainsay that a Christian's calling entailed fundamental conflict with the political order insofar as Rome required its subjects to recognize the absolute supremacy of political rule and, in this sense, to worship the emperor. In accord with Wolin's analysis, therefore, one might say that the Christian confession had revolutionary political import. As the witness of some early Christians confirms, however, martyrdom, rather than a deliberate attempt to reshape the character of political rule, was the proper course when political demands violated Christian faith, because the moral focus was on the different life within the new society. Summarily speaking, then, the early Christian self-understanding did not include a common political vocation.

This understanding, some have proposed, was dictated in part by political impotence. "The early Christian community was made up of scattered groups without political power" and thus could have no realistic "sense of responsibility for the organization of society" (Knox: 31). Moreover, awareness that forms of social stratification and political order were largely immune to change was apparently widespread in the empire and conditioned "what is usually called the growing individualism of late Hellenistic ethics" (Meeks: 28).

Probably of greater significance to early Christian self-understanding, formed as it was in the context of Jewish apocalyticism, was the expectation of an imminent divine ending to the present worldly order.[3] "The interim before the kingdom of God should come was so short that any acceptance of responsibility for society was out of the question. The situation was not that social responsibility of this kind was considered but, then, on reflection, rejected; it did not come into view at all, even as a possibility. God was going to deal with the social order; he was going to do so decisively and soon" (Knox: 59–60). Even if we suppose that Paul saw the revolutionary import of the gospel, for instance, his own commitment to an imminent eschatology made that recognition irrelevant.

As decades and then centuries passed, this expectation proved to be misguided, and as the fifth century of the Common Era emerged, Augustine chastised those who ask when the worldly order will end: "It is vain, therefore, that we try to reckon and put a limit to the number of years that remain for this world, since we hear from the mouth of the Truth that it is not for us to know this" (Augustine 1984: 838).[4] During these same centuries, nonetheless, something like Paul's apparent understanding of how Christians generally should relate to the political order became the prevailing view, at least in the following sense: The Roman monarchy and its political institutions were themselves under God's control and thus to be obeyed, if not honored. The peace and order they provided, however coercively, were thought to be essential both to human life and to the purpose of the church. In the second century, Irenaeus held that "power on earth was established by God for men's benefit, not by the devil"; in the third century, Origen "held that emperors ruled by divine right and that monarchy was the best form of government"; and the fourth-century apologist, Eusebius, "interpreted the history of the empire as proving the superiority of monarchy to any kind of state with more than one ruler" (Grant: 30, 32, 34). The church's alliance with Constantine and the favored status Christianity thereby enjoyed in the empire reinforced this understanding. To be sure, Christian thinkers had ample

---

3. Apocalyptic sects, pervasive in the Jewish religious context in which Christianity arose, typically believed that a certain seer, through whose vision a given sect began, was instructed by God to announce the imminent end of the age and to exhort people to prepare for it. For an account of this context, see Marxsen: 64–8.

4. Unless otherwise noted, citations from Augustine are from Augustine 1984, *The City of God* and will henceforth be by page number alone.

grounds on which to distinguish between better and worse political rulers and often formulated moral standards to which the monarchy and its magistrates were bound. Typically, however, conceptions of proper rule were advanced as exhortations or counsels to rulers. Thus, if church leaders should sometimes speak in this way to the king or his agents, that responsibility was not part of a common Christian vocation to help shape or pursue change within the larger society. To the contrary, most Christians were called or, at least, permitted to be politically accommodating or quiescent.

Henceforth, I will call this prescription the "early account" of political responsibility. On one reading of his monumental achievement, Augustine gave this account its most comprehensive early statement. During his leadership, the church no longer occupied the marginal social position characteristic of first-century Christians, and, as mentioned, he did not share Paul's expectation of an imminent eschaton. Nonetheless, Augustine also focused the social attention of Christians on the character and extension of their distinctive community, because he, in his own way, also understood the church to be an eschatological community. The City of God, "or rather that part of it which is on pilgrimage in this condition of mortality, ... leads what we may call a life of captivity in this earthly city." Naturally, "this mortal condition is shared by both cities" and, therefore, "a harmony may be preserved between them in things relevant to this condition" (877). But the lives of all within the earthly city are made miserable by their participation in original sin. The state and other principal institutions of this city are God's provision for the conditions of fallen existence, designed to regulate "those things" required for "the support of this mortal life" (877) and thus to provide a measure of peace and stability in circumstances that would otherwise be characterized by unrestrained strife.

The "Heavenly City" is only on pilgrimage in this world because its completion, to which those humans belonging to it are destined, is in eternity. "Life will only be truly happy when it is eternal" (590), that is, when a human is resurrected into "that commonwealth whose founder and ruler is Christ" (75), the "City of God which is . . . eternally immortal in heaven" (463). Blessedness consists in "the untroubled enjoyment of the changeless Good, which is God, together with the certainty of remaining in him for eternity" (444) and cannot be achieved under the conditions of sin. Augustine can even say that "this life is a calamity to be deplored" because "the other [eternal life] is the felicity for which we should long" (1067). Captive within these conditions, the "Heavenly City.... takes no account of any difference in customs, laws, and institutions, by which earthly peace is achieved and preserved – not that she annuls or abolishes any of those, rather, she maintains them and follows them . . . , provided that no hindrance is presented thereby to the religion which teaches that the one supreme and true God is to be worshiped" (878). Given that this last condition is met, the institutions of social and political order are finally of no importance for those who seek to live here according to "the standard of God" (552).

To be sure, the commandment that "a man who loves God" should also love "his neighbor" includes the rules "to do no harm to anyone, and, secondly, to help everyone whenever possible." But it means above all to "be concerned also that his neighbor should love God," just as "he will wish his neighbor to be concerned with him, if he happens to need that concern" (873). Christians who belong to the City of God during its captivity anticipate and prepare for eternity within the Christian community, and love for the neighbor, whether within or without that community, means especially the concern that she or he, too, should live with true piety – a life for which temporal goods have value only insofar as they serve to sustain and express the belief that they have no final importance. In sum, the meaning of Christian faith separates "earthly peace," which the political order maintains, from the "heavenly peace" of "the perfectly ordered and completely harmonious fellowship in the enjoyment of God, and of each other in God" (878). This difference so defines the relation between Christian faith and political community as to authorize the early account of political responsibility. For "what does it matter under whose rule a man lives, being so soon to die, provided that the rulers do not force him to impious and wicked acts" (205)?

Augustine does not deny moral norms for the regulation of things necessary to this mortal life and affirms standards for rulers that leaders of the church could or should proclaim. Further, "there is no happier situation for mankind" than one in which "those who are endowed with true piety" and "are skilled in the art of government" also "wield power" (213–14). But even rulers corrupted by "the passion for domination" are given power "by the providence of God," when God decides that man's condition deserves such masters (213).

On this reading, Augustine prescribed for Christians "a solemn duty to obey the laws and commands of the rulers.... They owe to rulers, no matter how wicked or tyrannical they may be, not only obedience and reverence but respect and love" (Deane: 143–4). This follows, negatively, because no earthly evil is worse than the strife consequent on the breakdown of social and political order and, positively, because the Heavenly City is only on pilgrimage here. Disobedience is prescribed only when laws or commands prohibit piety or present a hindrance to the true religion, such as a command to worship idols. But Augustine "never argues that the Christian has a right not to be punished when he refuses to obey a law or an order of this kind" (Deane: 147), much less to rebel against authority or seek to change the political order. The proper course is "to follow the example of the holy martyrs" (Deane: 149) and, thereby, to accept earthly rule as ordained by God even while preserving allegiance to a higher power. The call to Christian faith does not include politics as a common vocation.

II ASSESSING THE EARLY ACCOUNT

The preceding summary of early Christian understandings suffers from its compressed character and is open to refinement or correction at several points. Still, it seems fair to say that what I have called the early account of political responsibility was, in its essential outline, widely shared during the centuries we have covered. In any event, my purpose in reaching that conclusion is simply to reinforce the significance of another question: Is the early account or something like it authoritative for contemporary Christian witness in relation to the political order? When Christians today ask what should be given to Caesar in order always to serve the divine purpose, are they to be guided by the prevailing view of early Christianity, at least in this respect: The governing authorities are divinely appointed and, therefore, most Christians are not called to be agents who seek to help determine social and political structures?

One possible response asserts that Paul himself misunderstood or misrepresented the meaning of Christian faith. On this view, we can discover in witness to the gospel that precedes even Paul the true political obligations of all Christians, namely, a political commitment to resist and reform unjust social and political structures. Something like this seems to be the position taken by some advocates of the social gospel in late-nineteenth- and early-twentieth-century America, who so interpreted biblical references to the kingdom of God. "The social gospel is, in fact, the oldest gospel of all," wrote Walter Rauschenbusch. "Its substance is the Hebrew faith which Jesus himself held. If the prophets ever talk about the 'plan of redemption,' they meant the social redemption of the nation," and Jesus, for whom "the Kingdom of God" was the "central word," proclaimed a gospel that "looked toward a higher social order in which new ethical standards would become practicable" (Rauschenbusch: 24).

In his own way, Rauschenbusch agrees with the summary reading we have given of early Christianity. For him, the Kingdom idea "shriveled" more or less immediately after the death of Jesus, as "groups of disciples joined and consolidated by inward necessity." Thereby, "the name and idea of 'the Kingdom' began to be displaced by the name and idea of 'the Church,'" understood as "the partial and earthly realization of the divine Society" that would "merge" with the Kingdom "at the Parousia." Augustine "completed this process in his *De Civitate Dei*." Only in the modern age has the Kingdom idea been revived, a retrieval indebted to "the combined influence of the historical study of the Bible and of the social gospel" (Rauschenbusch: 132, 133). On some readings, a relevantly similar response to the early account may be found in some formulations of later-twentieth-century liberation theology.

I will not pursue the extended appraisal this view merits. Setting it aside does not imply a challenge to the social gospel or relevantly similar forms of liberation theology as contemporary explications of the Christian faith. My doubt is only that any successful defense of them could include the kind of appeal by which the Christian community from Paul to Augustine is charged with the fundamental mistake Rauschenbusch asserts.[5] Assuming room for such doubt, I will pass over the indictment because I seek to clarify politics as a

---

5. As supposedly based on what Jesus said or meant, this indictment is, I believe, untenable because we cannot distinguish within our sources the deeds and words of the so-called historical Jesus from the way in which the earliest Christian witness to him represented his significance. Nor can the indictment be authorized by that earliest witness itself. Its essence, so far as I can judge, was its proclamation of God's call to faith and did not include a directive regarding political responsibility. For a

Christian vocation while crediting wherever possible the principal representatives of Christian thought and practice inherited by the contemporary church. Accordingly, the discussion here will assume that the early account was in some substantial sense a fitting expression of the Christian faith.

A second response is consistent with this assumption: The view Paul apparently took and to which Augustine, at least on one reading of him, gave the most comprehensive statement was fitting by virtue of the particular context in which early Christians were called to determine their relation to politics. Thus, political accommodation is an application within that context of the abiding Christian calling and may not be fitting in altered circumstances. There is also a third response: Contrary to the second, the particular context is largely inconsequential, because something very like the view of political responsibility we have reviewed belongs to the abiding content of Christian faith. Given the dramatic differences between the Roman Empire and modern political conditions, we may assume that the early account can have authority today only if the essential meaning of Christian faith includes or implies it. What is of the essence, those who so believe may assert, is this: Love of God and neighbor, while surely expressed in personal or individual relations with all people, pursues a transformed order of human interaction principally within the Christian community, so that larger social structures may and, perhaps, should be left to God's control. Hence, Christians do not have a common political vocation, except when the governing authorities present a hindrance to the church and its practice of true religion.

So understood, the third response has found favor in the history of the church. This may become more apparent if we underscore that, as the early martyrs imply and as Augustine explicitly says, the early account instructs Christians to disobey the political order when it interferes with their community's distinctive task – and if we then allow that disobedience may, in some historical circumstances, include political activity that seeks to remove the hindrance. Working with some such broad interpretation, we can, I believe, see this account throughout the medieval period and in some expressions of the

discussion of these matters on which my own understandings are dependent, see Ogden 1982.

Reformation, although the different qualifications with which the early centuries are appropriated are also significant.[6] Moreover, the history of Christian thought more or less continuous with early political accommodation extends into our contemporary context. Something like the third response is affirmed by many Christians today, and I will return to this fact in Chapter 5. Further review here of the historical record would postpone unnecessarily the principal purposes of this work, which concern Christians today. Even without greater detail, however, we can say that Christians for whom politics is a common Christian vocation differ with a profound tradition in Christian thought and practice, and the question this difference occasions may be reformulated: Does the early account belong to the abiding content of Christian faith or does it apply that faith to particular political contexts?

In taking up that question, we plainly require some norm or standard by which the abiding content of Christian faith can be properly determined and disagreements about it adjudicated. Some may object, moreover, that meeting this need depends on a prior assumption, namely, that Christian faith in fact has an abiding content, a meaning that is essential to it or by which it is properly defined in all historical situations. Certain modern thinkers, attentive to the historical contingency of all human expressions, have doubted or denied any such essence. But this objection, I believe, is confused and should be rejected for the following reason: The denial of any permanent meaning to Christian faith contradicts the confession that Christians respond to God's revelation through Jesus Christ. If there is no abiding content and thus only many meanings of Christian faith, Jesus cannot have the decisive importance claimed in asserting that he is the Christ. To help make this point persuasive, we should distinguish an abiding content, on the one hand, from appropriate statements or

---

6. The Introduction to this work noted that the use of "vocation" was transformed by the Reformation. Having been reserved in the medieval Christian community to mean specifically religious activities, the term came to mean for Protestants any honest and useful work as an occasion for witness to God's presence. Given this meaning, politics might now be a Christian vocation. But this change itself does not make politics a *common* Christian vocation. Just as, in earlier centuries, Christian leaders might have been given the responsibility to exhort or counsel rulers (and, indeed, a Christian might be a ruler), so Protestants could believe that particular Christians might have a political vocation. In continuity with the early account, however, Reformation thought typically did not consider active participation in politics a responsibility to which Christians generally are called.

formulations of it, on the other. Many who find the objection troubling are, I suspect, mindful that these formulations are subject to change in view of changed social and cultural conditions. But affirming that Christian faith has an essential meaning is quite consistent with agreeing that appropriate statement of it depends on the peculiarities of a given historical setting. The relevant point, then, is that differing statements may all be appropriate because they express the same content.

Still, disagreements about the essential meaning of Christian faith are the more difficult to adjudicate because Christians have also disagreed and continue to differ, both in principle and in fact, about what counts as the primary norm to which expressions of the faith should conform. Most of Christian history has asserted that this norm is the apostolic witness to Jesus as the Christ, but there has been disagreement about what is in fact apostolic, some equating this with the New Testament canon or, alternatively, the essential "biblical message" contained within the canon, and others affirming as apostolic both Scripture and tradition. More recently, some theologians have, in effect, denied the principle of apostolicity itself, insisting that the primary norm of Christian faith consists in the words and deeds of the so called historical Jesus. Although every solution to this problem has its own difficulties, I am persuaded by Schubert M. Ogden that the least problematic account contrasts with all of the preceding views. Each of them, Ogden argues, conflicts with the principle on which the church determined the New Testament canon itself, namely, that primary authority belongs to writings authored by the apostles as witnesses to Jesus. Since more than two centuries of modern biblical study have now shown that the canonical writings were mistakenly thought to be apostolic and were, in truth, dependent on earlier sources, the relatively more adequate solution today takes as the primary norm of Christian faith the earliest Christian witness behind the New Testament texts and available through historical-critical study of them (see Ogden 1982: 96–105).

I will not seek to defend that solution here. For present purposes, I propose to avoid the extensive discussion proper address to the problem must involve by invoking a minimal assumption about the content of Christian faith that I take to command widespread assent among Christians notwithstanding their disagreement about the norm by which it is authorized. This assumption has two inseparable aspects. First, I assume, in keeping with some earlier comments, that the call to love God with all one's heart and soul and mind and strength, and thus one's neighbor as oneself, is finally the only Christian commandment, in the sense that all others are applications or articulations of it. Second, I assume that this commandment comes to Christians with the revelation of God's prior love through Jesus Christ. Jesus is the Christ because he is the one through whom the saving love of God for all the world is decisively revealed, so that Christian faith means entrusting oneself completely to salvation by the God Jesus reveals and, thereby, embracing the commandment given with God's love.

In proposing this interpretation, I do not imply that it expresses the meaning of Christian faith *because* it commands widespread agreement among Christians. To the contrary, no such interpretation can be authorized except by the primary norm of Christian faith. My intent here is simply to presume that a proper interpretation will include this assumed content, recognizing that any subsequent conclusions based on it cannot be fully established without returning to validate the assumption. Allowing the discussion to proceed in this way, we can accept the following summary statement: The call through Jesus to love without reservation the God who loves all the world defines the abiding content of Christian faith, in the sense that anything else belonging to its essence must be everywhere consistent with this calling. No other meaning essential to Christian belief, in other words, can be in any circumstances inconsistent with the Great Commandment given with God's love.[7] To be sure, many disagreements can and do arise in spelling out those other meanings. That is the sense in which the assumption is a minimal one. If we here leave those disagreements aside, the question we must now seek to address may

---

7. In a formal sense, this norm is similar to a criterion for being human; for instance, anything belonging to the essential meaning of being human must be everywhere consistent with being self-conscious or potentially self-conscious. On this criterion, being a Roman citizen cannot belong to the essential meaning of being human, since this specific feature is not consistent with, for instance, the contemporary self-consciousness of a Japanese citizen. I also note that the norm offered here is meant explicitly to mark only a necessary condition of essential Christian meaning. That a given belief is not in all circumstances consistent with the Great Commandment entails that it cannot belong to the abiding content of Christian faith. Is abiding consistency with the Great Commandment a sufficient condition of essential Christian meaning, so that any belief having this feature belongs to the abiding content? That is another question, which I here intend to leave open, because I mean the norm to be a minimal one.

again be reformulated: Is the early account of political responsibility everywhere consistent with unreserved love for the God revealed through Jesus Christ or is that account an application of that love to particular historical circumstances?

III THE MODERN DIFFERENCE

Those for whom the early account, broadly understood, expresses something essential might insist that grounds for their conviction are eminently given in Augustine's achievement, briefly reviewed earlier. The separation of "earthly peace" and "heavenly peace" is fundamental to Christian faith. Since the church is the eschatological community, moral concern is properly focused on this community of higher purpose itself, and political rule is accepted as the provision of God's providence during the pilgrimage in this earthly city of Christians who are destined for the eternal commonwealth. Politics is not a common Christian vocation.

Thorough assessment of this defense would require a theological argument of the same comprehensive order as Augustine's gift to us, attending especially to his understanding of God's relation to the world and thus of the Trinity and the redemption from sin effected by incarnation of the Word in the man, Jesus. In subsequent chapters, I will argue that some aspects of this understanding fail adequately to express the meaning of Christian faith. But even without that assessment, we may still question whether an appreciation of Augustine requires contemporary Christians to concede abiding authority to the early account. I do not deny that his separation between eternity and time, if appropriate to Christian faith, readily supports moral focus on the City of God within this earthly city as the abiding Christian calling. But another belief is also central to Augustine, and when we consider its implications, they will suggest a way for contemporary Christians to honor his achievement even while entertaining a departure from the early account.

Although he insists that true happiness or felicity occurs only in the eternal commonwealth to which temporal goods have no final importance, Augustine gives no cause for a person who loves God to be indifferent toward the want of worldly good or the suffering of worldly evil. To the contrary, a Christian "will be at peace, as far as lies in him, with all men" and will, as we have noted, seek to observe two rules: "first, to do no harm to anyone, and, secondly, to help everyone whenever possible" (873). These rules prescribe a concern "for the interests of others," which include "certain good things suitable to this life," namely, "the peace that consists in bodily health and soundness, and in fellowship with one's kind; and everything necessary to safeguard and recover this peace" (874, 872) – even if pursuing worldly goods as though they provided true felicity sacrifices "the Supreme Good" and embraces "the Supreme Evil" (852). Moreover, the counsel to accept and obey the laws and orders of political rulers is itself an expression of a Christian's proper concern for the interests of all, because the worst evil of this world is civil disorder and strife, and a true Christian who has the opportunity to be a ruler and the skill to govern is obligated to accept the exercise of power (see 219–20).

The central point is that this world and life within it, however deformed by sin, are God's creation and, therefore, good. "There is only one cause for the creation of the world – the purpose of God's goodness in the creation of good." Thus, "if no one had sinned in the world, the world would have been furnished and fitted only with things naturally good" (455). Sin notwithstanding, moreover, Augustine speaks often of the world's beauty. Presented to our sight, it "bears a kind of silent testimony ... that its maker could have been none other than God" (432; see also 475). But its beauty also extends far beyond our limited appreciation. "A picture may be beautiful when it has touches of black in appropriate places; in the same way the whole universe is beautiful, if one could see it as a whole, even with its sinners, though their ugliness is disgusting when they are viewed in themselves" (455–6; see also 449). For Augustine, in other words, all things "tend, in God's plan, to that end which is included in the whole design for the government of the universe" (476). However hidden from our limited comprehension, everything contributes to a whole of the greatest possible beauty.

For this reason, "there is no such entity in nature as 'evil'; 'evil' is merely a name for the privation of good" (454) or for "the loss of good" (440) – just as, Augustine often says, sin has no efficient cause but, rather, a "deficient" cause (481). A defective will, he explains, "can only exist in a nature which God created out of *nothing*, not in that nature which the Creator begot out of himself, as he begot the

Word through which all things are made" (568, emphasis added), even while "the *choice* of evil is an impressive proof that the *nature* is good" (448). Because God's creation is good, love for or attachment to "what is destined to come into being" through "the disappearance of mutable and mortal natures" (476–7) cannot exclude concern for the worldly interests of "everyone whenever possible," and Christian faith sanctions as a good of this "mortal life" such "harmonious agreement of citizens" (877) as is possible – however impossible it may also be fully to know how the creation makes its contribution to the eternal commonwealth. Whatever else may or may not belong to the abiding content of Christian faith, I will assume, Augustine's affirmation of the world as God's creation of good must be included. It is everywhere consistent with and, further, implied by unreserved love for the God of all-embracing love because the goodness of the world follows directly from God's love for it.

With this belief in mind, let us return to whether Augustine's thought entails abiding authority for the early account. If the difference between earthly and heavenly peace does not permit indifference to worldly conditions in which neighbors and fellow citizens live, why is political accommodation prescribed or, at least, permitted for most Christians? We can take for granted that political rule has far-ranging consequences for worldly good and evil. How, then, could commitment to the earthly good of everyone exclude a common political vocation marked by resistance to injustice and active pursuit of a better political order? We have already noted at least one answer to this question, namely, the judgment that civil disorder and strife is the worst evil that can invade the earthly city, so that nonresistance to the governing authorities *is* an expression of one's commitment to earthly good. Let us grant that Augustine had sound reasons for this view. In the context of our present discussion, we must now ask whether his judgment is valid in all times and places or, to the contrary, is true only given certain conditions of the earthly city. When one says that resistance to injustice threatens greater evil than good, has one described an abiding aspect of human life together or, instead, issued a warning whose validity depends on certain specific social and political circumstances? If the latter, then the early account, insofar as it derives from that judgment, does not belong to the abiding content of Christian faith but is, rather, an attempt to specify the life of Christian witness to a particular situation.

Consider the differing conditions within a modern community that has, or at least approaches, a democratic form of government. In that setting, the process through which legal order, its interpretation, and its enforcement are determined somehow legitimates as active participants all those who are thereby governed or ruled. Thus, deliberate attempts by Christians to effect justice within the political community may be, at least if pursued in accord with constitutionally defined procedures, so far from a threat to disorder as to be the very nature of citizenship. Given a commitment to serve the worldly good of "everyone, whenever possible," it is far from apparent that the early account is fitting. Having in mind these contemporary conditions, in which active pursuit of justice need not be anarchic, let us examine further why Augustine's affirmation of earthly good did not lead him to affirm politics as a common Christian vocation.

It will not suffice to stress that pervasive sin severely limits the possibilities of justice, since there is always the possibility of better rather than worse political rule. The most apparent answer, rather, is this: In the circumstances of the Roman Empire, it was beyond question that rule must be by the one or the few and, further, that the mechanisms for choosing the one or the few themselves involved at most the few. Rule by the many, meaning that they participate in the selection of rulers and, in some way, can be active in shaping the exercise of power, was not a real possibility. Accordingly, it did not come into view as an alternative to be assessed in light of the calling to love God without reservation and, therefore, one's neighbor as oneself. Under these conditions, a refusal to accept the political order and obey its rulers had no realistic expression except passive disengagement, on the one hand, and, on the other, some form of rebellion that is, in the nature of the case, disorderly and violent. Whatever the implications of Augustine's separation between earthly and heavenly peace, I expect that his irrevocable belief in God as creator of the world would not have permitted his assertion of the early account in the absence of these circumstances.[8]

8. There is another defense of the early account in Augustine. Under the conditions of sin, the many are not fit to rule and, therefore, rule should be by one or the few who are more capable of watching over the common good (see, for instance, Augustine 1993: 10–11). I doubt that this defense would have been persuasive to Augustine absent the circumstances of the Roman Empire, although anything approaching certainty in such judgments is impossible. In any case, I will discuss political

III. The Modern Difference

Within many modern communities, however, rule by the many is not only possible but also, in some significant manner, established. Consider again a political community in which democratic ideals are not merely an ideological cover for dictatorial control or the monopoly power of a privileged elite; that is, citizens generally have a real opportunity to help shape the political order. For the moment, let us also assume that Christian faith prescribes or, at least, does not prohibit democracy as a form of government – recognizing that this assumption will require attention in subsequent chapters. Given the profound consequences of political rule for worldly good and evil, circumstances now imply that active resistance to political wrongs and deliberate pursuit of justice belong to the vocation of Christians generally because they are called to help "everyone, whenever possible" or to love their neighbors as themselves. But, then, the essence of Christian faith cannot include the early account of political responsibility because, at least under the conditions described, political quiescence is not consistent with unreserved love for the God who loves all the world. Accordingly, the early account must be an application to the particular context in which rule by the many was not possible. However fitting that specification was within the social and political circumstances of early Christians and, further, for subsequent Christians whose situation was similar in relevant respects, the prescription that most Christians may or should be politically accommodating cannot be authoritative for all circumstances of Christian witness.

To be sure, this assessment of the early account may itself depend on or be aided by conditions that differ from those of the early church. If the circumstances in which Augustine prescribed politically for Christians precluded rule by the many, perhaps it was also difficult at best to anticipate a future state of affairs in which such rule could occur. This is not to say that early Christians thinkers were unfamiliar with politics in which many participate, since it was one of the forms practiced in classical Greek city-states and assessed by classical Greek thinkers, even if its conception differed from modern democratic ideas. Still, the development of ancient empires, and especially the Roman Empire, effectively erased this possibility with the ending

accommodation based on the idea of political inequality in the next chapter, attending to Aquinas's formulation of that view.

of city-states as independent political units. However vulnerable the empire itself was during Augustine's life, there may have been no realistic expectation of a return to classical Greek conditions. In these circumstances, one might argue, altered conditions in which the early account would no longer be fitting could not themselves come into view, and Christian thinkers might readily conclude that their determination of political responsibility belonged to the abiding content of Christian faith. If this is so, then perhaps a conclusion to the contrary itself waited on a change in social and political circumstances.

Nonetheless, excluding the early account from essential Christian belief may still be correct. To distinguish the abiding content of Christian faith from its application to variable circumstances is not to imply that clarity about what belongs to the one and what to the other must itself be abiding. Those who insist on the distinction have no reason to deny that possible or presumable understandings of the one in difference from the other may themselves depend on variable conditions. The changing circumstances of Christian thought include not only differing social and political institutions but also differing cultural and conceptual resources in terms of which those institutions and, more generally, the distinction between abiding and variable contents of Christian faith are interpreted. For this reason, Christians having the advantage of later social and cultural circumstances may be able to see that earlier thinkers were, in some given respect, mistaken about the essence of Christian belief – however justified, given their circumstances, their formulations may have been.

Let us assume, for instance, that Paul counseled political accommodation in part because he foresaw an imminent divine end to the current worldly order. Assume, further, that he thought this anticipation an essential aspect of Christian belief. Although Augustine prescribed substantially the same political responsibility, he also rejected Paul's imminent eschatology, asserting from the advantage of later circumstance that humans cannot know "the number of years remaining for this world" (838). Perhaps this denial of Paul's accounting did not require Augustine to fault Paul and his contemporaries, given that their formulations of Christian self-understanding occurred within the cultural and conceptual resources of Jewish apocalypticism. In a similar manner, then, contemporary Christians need not fault Augustine if they conclude, having the advantage of altered political and cultural conditions, that he was mistaken about the abiding political responsibilities of Christians.[9] To the contrary, they may honor his achievement notwithstanding that they rightly claim an advance in understanding the essence of Christian faith.

Still, our discussion has not yet shown that early Christian thinkers were mistaken about the abiding political responsibilities of Christians. What we have said warrants that conclusion only if the modern circumstances in which democracy is established or approached make a difference to how Christian witness relates to politics. Whether or not this is so is the question that will now occupy our attention.

---

9. In order to avoid misunderstanding, I emphasize that nothing said here denies an abiding content to Christian faith. Perhaps that denial now seems implied, not because appropriate formulation depends on social and cultural circumstances but, rather, because distinguishing the abiding content to be formulated from its variable applications does or may also depend on those circumstances. Were there this implication, however, there would be no distinction to explicate. Given an essential meaning to Christian faith, which I take to be implied by the confession of Jesus as the Christ, later circumstances may, in certain respects, offer an advantage in giving that meaning more adequate statement, thereby permitting the recognition that earlier formulations were mistaken. To be sure, Christians for whom the early account is inapplicable in our setting may also concede that political quiescence could again become fitting in some future context of life. But this does not mean that present Christians are wrong about their early predecessors. If the early account is not applicable in present circumstances, it cannot belong to the faith's abiding content in any situation.

Chapter 2

Government by the People

Christians today cannot simply assume that the early account has abiding authority for their political responsibilities. Given modern conditions that are or approach being democratic, the situation in which unreserved love for God and neighbor relates to politics has altered dramatically, raising the question of whether the view dominating Christian thought from Paul to Augustine was, in one way or another, an application of Christian belief dependent on social and culture circumstances peculiar to the time. Contrary to that tradition, Christians in modern circumstances that are or approach being democratic may be commonly called to political activity for justice and the common good. Still, the discussion to this point has not shown that politics today is a common Christian vocation. As we noted, the difference between modern democracy and early Christian political conditions does not warrant departure from the early account unless Christian faith prescribes or, at least, does not prohibit democracy as a form of government, and we are some considerable distance from a successful defense of that conclusion.

Indeed, there is another defense of the early account. Whatever the distinct conditions of modern life, one might say, Christians are not commonly called to political activity because, under those conditions as everywhere else, Christian faith asserts the inherent political inequality of human beings and prescribes rule by the one or the few. Some early Christian thinkers, we have noted, affirmed monarchy as the best form of government, and Augustine at least took it for granted. Naturally, this view might also be explained in terms of the social and cultural circumstances of the Roman Empire. But any such explanation assumes rather than shows the absence of this affirmation within the abiding content of Christian faith. To the contrary, as we will pursue in a moment, an abiding principle of monarchical or aristocratic rule was advanced and defended by Thomas Aquinas, based on what he took to be the natural inequality among human individuals – and some might well hold that he articulated a position Augustine shared.[1]

For most contemporary Christians, no doubt, this position does not merit a serious hearing. Still, calling it to mind serves to underscore that conclusions about Christian vocations depend finally on the meaning of Christian faith. Perhaps believing that Christian faith endorses or, at least, does not oppose democratic politics seems noncontroversial. But doing so uncritically may fail to clarify the understanding of Christian commitment by which democracy is authorized. Although I share the belief, setting forth the grounds for it is, as I hope will become apparent, profoundly important for articulating politics as a Christian vocation.

Asking how Christian witness relates to democracy involves two other questions: First, what political principles, or principles of justice and the common good, are included in or implied by Christian faith? Without an answer to this first question, one cannot begin to determine what form or forms of government Christian witness affirms. Second, what is the character of a democratic political community? Without identifying its distinguishing features, one cannot determine whether it is prescribed or even permitted by a Christian understanding of justice and the common good. In this chapter, I will seek to address the second of these two questions, postponing the first for later discussion. As I will seek to show, precision about democracy will also explicate the basis for its assertion of political equality. Thereby, we will clarify the commitment Christian faith must require or allow its contemporary adherents to accept if they are rightly to affirm, against Aquinas or any other, popular political participation. It will be useful to begin with a brief account of Aquinas's position and then to outline how democracy emerged in the modern period.

---

1. Whether political inequality is said to be an aspect of our created natures as humans or, instead, a consequence of original sin (see Chapter 1, footnote 8) does not affect the inconsistency I will explicate between democracy and political inequality.

I POPULAR SOVEREIGNTY

The transparent difference between politics during the early centuries of Christianity and within the contemporary context is, we have said, the modern emergence of rule by the many. This contrast serves further as a summary comparison of modern democracy and the previous Western political tradition as a whole, at least during the Common Era. However divergent its many expressions, this tradition sustained an overwhelming consensus that political rule properly belongs to one or the few, who should have power because of their uncommon wisdom or virtue or because they are divinely appointed. However fitfully, modern democracy has turned its back on this legacy.

The premodern consensus was typically authorized, at least throughout the medieval period, by a view of reality as ordered and united through a hierarchy of beings.[2] Like so many other characteristic medieval understandings, this one received preeminent formulation from Aquinas. Repeating Augustine's view that the universe is divinely designed and ordered in eternity, Aquinas saw all things unified in terms of their ends or purposes as defined by the eternal purpose or eternal law of God. Unity consists in a predetermined gradation of beings, stretching from the earthly elements through living creatures to the heavenly bodies and angels, such that "God through the order of His providence directs lower beings by means of higher ones" (S.C.G. 3.146.2; see also 3.77–9).[3] Since, for Aquinas, an ordering cause must include whatever becomes actual in its effects, higher beings include and surpass the perfection of lower ones, just as in God "all the perfections of things pre-exist excellently" (S.T. 1.13.5).

Within this order of ends ranking all things, the political community itself includes individuals who are by nature unequal in their capacities. Hence, its permanently proper structure is stratified or hierarchical. Just as "in natural things, it behooved the higher to move the lower to their actions by the excellence of the natural power bestowed on them by God, ... so, in human affairs also, the higher should move the lower by their will in virtue of divinely established authority" (S.T. 2–2.104.1). Political rule, then, properly belongs to

---

2. The discussion in this section is especially indebted to Samuel H. Beer (see Beer).

3. Citations from Aquinas's *Summa Contra Gentiles* (S.C.G.) designate in order the number of the book, the chapter, and the paragraph. The translations I have used are noted in Works Cited.

those whose capacity for wisdom and virtue includes and surpasses all others. "Political prudence, which is directed to the common good of the political community" (S.T. 2–2.47.1), is a virtue of those who are ruled, and "rulers' prudence is the most perfect species of prudence" (S.T. 2–2.50.2 ad 1). Although he may not have been completely consistent on the point, Aquinas characteristically defended monarchy or "the rule of one man" as "unqualifiedly the best" (*On Kingship*: 6).[4] "A social life cannot exist among a number of people unless under the governance of one to look after the common good; for many, as such, seek many things, whereas one attends to only one" (ST 1.103.1).

Aquinas did hold that the king or other rulers are bound by the natural law and thus bound to rule justly. Should the human or civil law effected by the ruler depart "at any point . . . from the law of nature . . . , it is no longer a law but a perversion of law" (S.T. 2–1.95.2). Accordingly, "the governance of a kingdom must be arranged so that there is no opportunity given for a king . . . to act as a tyrant" (*On Kingship*: 6), and, "if the prince's authority is not just . . . or if he commands what is unjust, his subjects are not bound to obey him, except perhaps accidentally, in order to avoid scandal or danger" (S.T. 2–2.104.6 ad 3). But the possible dangers are considerable. In distinction from Augustine, Aquinas allowed a right to revolution, through which the community seeks to change its rulers. Still, the occasions on which that course would be proper are apparently rare, and, in most cases, "even if he [the king] does become a tyrant, this should be tolerated so that greater evils can be avoided" (*On Kingship*: 6). Exceptional situations aside, then, subjects in general properly consent to and obey rule by one or the few because the many are not fit for political decisions and thus should defer to those whose superior capacity carries their right to power. Accordingly, one may say that Aquinas has more in common than in difference with Augustine's prescription for acceptance of and obedience to the governing authorities.

The understanding of reality and the human community as stratified continued to influence political thought into the early modern period, for instance, in the writings of the "judicious" Richard Hooker, against whom John Locke crafted much of his two treatises on government (see Beer: 58–60). As the reference to Locke suggests, however,

---

4. Citations from Aquinas's *On Kingship* designate the chapter. The translation I have used is noted in Works Cited.

the modern democratic alternative began to take shape in the seventeenth century through the work of English constitutionalists. We need not pursue a detailed review of this development. The central point concerns its increasing rejection of natural human inequality in the sense that defines a hierarchy of capacities and deference by the many to one or the few. In contrast to that belief, English thinkers in various ways affirmed "the subversive idea that the ordinary individual could contribute to the discovery of the common good by his own rational powers" (Beer: 64) and, accordingly, should have an active part in the determination of governmental activities. One of the earliest statements of this "subversive idea" appeared in John Milton's *Areopagitica*, where his "defense of liberty of conscience also makes the case for government by discussion" (Beer: 66), meaning that the best government occurs through free debate among those ruled by it.

Important as these English constitutionalists were, we would err in thinking that modern democracy is mainly the result of effective new ideas such as theirs. To the contrary, several students of political history have emphasized the unintended consequences of religious wars that, following the breakup of Christendom in the Protestant Reformation, devastated Europe in the late sixteenth and early seventeenth centuries. In pursuit of a stable peace, the response was a widespread call for religious toleration and thus for a form of government acceptable to differing religious communities. Thereby, the liberty of conscience and appeal to discussion Milton defended were given substantial reinforcement. Moreover, democracy emerged against the background of larger cultural and social changes, without which government by discussion probably would not have become a realistic proposal, and mention of this larger background will contribute to a proper conception of democratic politics.

The medieval view of reality and human life was inseparable, as in the case of Aquinas, from the authority of the Catholic Church. The metaphysical ranking of all things and the corresponding rule by one or the few were dependent on the Christian understanding of eternity and time of which the church was the final guarantor. Both the Renaissance and the Reformation, in their differing ways, challenged this cultural complex, as did, with increasing effect, the development of modern empirical science. As modernity progressed, the most basic cultural change was the increasing affirmation of reason as alone sufficient to validate understandings of reality and the human good and thus the increasing rejection of religious authority as necessary for knowing principles of belief and practice – a course that culminated in the eighteenth-century Enlightenment or so-called Age of Reason. Because the credibility of medieval metaphysics was so tied to religious authority, the modern affirmation of reason was largely inseparable from a discrediting of hierarchical metaphysics, especially given the modern scientific conviction that facts of the world could be explained solely in terms of empirical causation by prior facts, independently of any teleological order.

Without the framework of an eternal unity, the grounds for taking social stratification to be natural or fixed eroded. As modernity continued, it gave rise to a sweeping consciousness of human historicity, which, among other things, understood the structures of community to be human creations and thus subject to transformation. That persuasion was both cause and consequence of the emerging bourgeois or commercial classes, who "engaged in stubborn, and ultimately victorious, conflict with the ecclesiastical and aristocratic rulers of the feudal-medieval world" (Niebuhr 1944: 1–2). These classes made their own contribution to the emergence of democracy, because they advocated economic liberty against the traditional forms of social power and soon sought to add "the political power of suffrage to their growing economic power" (Niebuhr 1944: 2). In addition, economic development brought more abundant material resources, which removed or promised to remove the necessity that most people live at the level of mere subsistence in order that the few might attend to higher matters. Together with this new economic setting, then, the new conception of political order as fundamentally open to human determination and, indispensable to both, the commitment to rational understandings of the world and human life provided a larger social and cultural context in which the idea of government by discussion or free debate could have effect.

But if this context supported profound changes in European political thought, the possibilities for democracy were uncommonly favorable in the so-called New World, where the distinctive affirmations of modern culture could be appropriated within conditions that, beyond all others, offered the chance to begin again. In part for this reason, the meaning of democracy reached eminent expression through some leaders of the eighteenth-century American

Revolution, notwithstanding their failure fully to honor or institutionalize their profession. Of the various ways in which their political convictions might be summarily characterized, perhaps none is so apt as the phrase "sovereignty of the people." To be sure, the meaning of "sovereignty," a term introduced into Western political thought in the sixteenth and seventeenth centuries in connection with the new nation-state, is disputed. For present purposes, however, these disputes can be avoided by taking popular sovereignty to mean, in the phrase impressed on the memory of the United States by Abraham Lincoln, government by the people.

The achievement of American revolutionaries was their unqualified assertion that those who are ruled are also the final ruling authority. According to Samuel H. Beer, this insistence made the conflict between England and its thirteen American colonies finally intractable. Whatever the considerable commonalities, England on the whole continued to grant sovereignty to Parliament and, at least in this respect, special authority still belonged to those characterized by superior virtue. In contrast, the "enormous claim" of American republicans "was that the many could act as this final judge and power" (Beer: 150; see chap. 4). In that claim, modernity's overthrow of the long Western commitment to rule by one or the few was, in speech if not in deed, completed. I will not attempt further to trace Beer's account. Our summary review of social and political changes behind the articulation of popular sovereignty has pursued only the following summary point: Other background developments were profoundly connected with the increasing modern appeal to reason in the court over which religious authority previously presided. That basic cultural change will prove to be important for clarifying what government by the people means.

II THE CONSTITUTIONAL TASK

Popular government, some have said, means that final authority is vested in neither one nor the few but, rather, in a written or unwritten constitution. But the "enormous claim" on behalf of the many is far more radical. The constitution is itself authorized by the people, as the opening words to the United States Constitution make clear: "We the people of the United States, . . . do ordain and establish this

Constitution." Hence, "the sovereignty of the people" means at least this: First, every member of the political community is sovereign over her or his assessment of actual and proposed governmental activities and thus of any political claim, in the sense that the state may not legitimately stipulate or dictate that assessment. Here, "political claim" means a claim for the justice of any actual or proposed activity of the state or for the validity of any norm or principle of justice. Second, the final political authority consists in the equal importance of every such person's sovereign assessment. Somewhat more briefly stated, then, popular sovereignty means that all members of the political community have an inalienable right to make or contest any political claim, or do so legitimately, and together as equals they are the final political authority.

Given this meaning of government by the people, the distinctive democratic challenge is to reach decision in common or "as one" from the diverse assessments of the many (see Beer: 150–1). Whatever changes in politics or political thought Western history may include, the abiding purpose of political rule is to create order by which the community as a whole is unified, and there cannot be many unifications of the whole. In the democratic case, the full measure of this task can be taken when we recognize that religious freedom is essential to popular sovereignty. We have already noted that early modern wars among religions were unintentionally but nonetheless profoundly consequential for the emergence of democratic politics, and most subsequent political communities in the West have sought in one way or another to be tolerant of religious differences they include. But religious freedom is not merely a historical necessity dictated by religious plurality. It is, rather, a principled necessity that follows from popular sovereignty. So understood, it helps to clarify the challenge to democracy.

To be sure, precisely what freedom religious freedom protects depends on the deeply controversial question of what, if anything, the term "religion" designates. Some argue that a general sense of the term has no useful function or, at least, cannot be defined independently of a particular culture to be understood or a particular question to be addressed. An attempt to examine this controversy would also take us beyond our need in the context of this work.[5] For present

---

5. I discuss the definition of "religion" in relation to the principle of religious freedom in Gamwell 1995: see chap. 2.

purposes, we may approach the point about democracy by starting from what has been said about the abiding content of the Christian religion. On the minimal assumption discussed in Chapter 1, the essence of Christian faith is given in or everywhere consistent with the following belief: All worth or importance has its ultimate ground in the God whom Jesus Christ reveals as all-embracing love, and thus humans are called to unreserved commitment to or love for this God.

Because this commitment is unreserved, it means that human life should have no other purpose than this one, in the sense that all others should be applications or articulations of it. Thus, the calling to love all the world or to treat all individuals as those whom God loves is meant to orient or be expressed in all human life. Generalizing from this account of Christian faith, we can say that any other religion, in the sense relevant to our discussion, includes some or other explicit conviction about the ultimate ground of worth for human life as such. For our discussion, in other words, a religious belief is distinguished from other kinds of belief by being an explicit answer to the question: What is the ultimate ground of worth, and what inclusive human purpose does it authorize? It then follows that two or more religions disagree or differ in substance when they differ on what this ground is and thus what should be the unreserved commitment of human life.

Freedom with respect to beliefs of this kind is the democratic necessity articulated in the principle of religious freedom. A conviction about the orientation of all human life includes or implies ultimate terms for assessing actual or proposed activities of the state. Since government by the people means that every member of the political community is sovereign over her or his assessment of every political claim, she or he must be free to decide what in truth are the ultimate terms of political assessment. As stated in the First Amendment to the United States Constitution, therefore, religious freedom prohibits an "established religion," that is, a religion endorsed by the state or officially associated with it. The government's unifying activities may never include teaching or support for teaching that any given belief about ultimate worth is true or false. An official conviction of this order would stipulate or dictate to all members of the political community something about the ultimate terms of political assessment and, thereby, contradict popular sovereignty.

As necessary to democratic government, we should note, religious freedom protects any explicit conviction about the ultimate terms of political assessment, and not solely those expressed in commonly recognized religious traditions of communities, for instance, in Buddhist or Christian or Islamic or Jewish traditions. Convictions that in other contexts of discussion might be called philosophical rather than religious are thereby included. Further, beliefs that in other contexts might be called secularistic rather than religious – for instance, those of certain Marxists or thoroughly American chauvinists – are, in the broad sense relevant here, religious, given only that each claims explicitly to define the proper orientation of all political purposes.

Moreover, we should not exclude from protection those for whom principles of justice do not derive from a single purpose for all human life or even those for whom justice has no universal character to which politics everywhere is accountable. At least for democratic purposes, "ultimate terms of political assessment" and "ultimate ground of worth" should be understood in extended senses that include such views. If someone holds that political assessments cannot appeal to universal principles, it remains that she or he cannot make a political claim without implying some ultimate terms of assessment, however nonuniversal these are taken to be. Thereby, some understanding of the ultimate ground of worth is also implied, namely, whatever it is that authorizes those ultimate terms. Accordingly, we can also say that every political claim implies, in the relevant sense, an "inclusive purpose" for human life, even if one denies that this is a single purpose and is, rather, only a plurality of proper aims, each of which is specific to a given realm of life or to a given community.

With respect to political assessments, in other words, all of these views are answers to the same distinct question that more commonly recognized religions also answer. Each, in its own way, serves for those who affirm it the same function, at least in their status as members of the final political authority. Hence, the meaning of "religion" should be so understood that the principle of religious freedom legitimates all such beliefs about the ultimate terms of political assessment and, thereby, protects the sovereignty of each citizen over her or his assessment of every political claim. But, now, if the many who together have final political authority are free with respect to this kind of belief, it follows that their legitimate diversity will or may include disagreements at the most fundamental level of political claims. Since government by the people requires common decision and action in spite of this fundamental diversity, we can see just how radical is the democratic task.

Indeed, first appearances might suggest that this challenge cannot be met. If religious differences lead to conflict over specific political decisions, how might the conflict be civilized or the parties united? Common decisions, in distinction from resolutions imposed by force, seem to require appeal to some common ground in terms of which the opposed political purposes might be commonly assessed. In the case of religiously based political disagreement, however, the conflict occurs with respect to the most fundamental grounds of assessment, so that nothing common is left to which appeal might be made in order to secure action-as-one. In sum, religious freedom seems to invite irresolvable political conflict. If democracy means the sovereignty of each citizen over every political claim, government by the people seems to be a civil war waiting to happen. How, then, is democracy possible? Articulating the contemporary political responsibility of Christians now requires that we determine whether this question has a credible answer.

Whatever else is involved, we have now asked about the proper character of a democratic constitution. Whether written or unwritten, a constitution, in the sense I intend here, defines the political process or form of government by stipulating the principle or set of principles in accord with which common political decision making occurs. A democratic constitution, then, defines how in principle "we the people" are united. It does not follow that all properly democratic constitutions must be identical in all respects. The principles in question might be exemplified in differing ways in differing historical circumstances. Still, if government by the people is possible, so too is some general constitutional character that differing democratic communities exemplify, and this is what we seek here. Hence, I will use "constitutional principles" and similar terms to mean both this general character and the provisions of a given constitution in which it is exemplified, without further attention to the difference. Because these principles define how the people act-as-one, explicit adherence to them also defines all members of the community in their status as participants in political rule. To clarify the proper character of a democratic constitution is, in other words, also to explicate the ethics of democratic citizenship, that is, the norms that define legitimate participation in the political process and to which all people as citizens should explicitly or deliberately adhere.

But a democratic constitution, as we said earlier, must itself be authorized by "we the people" because they are the final political authority. Accordingly, the challenge might again be restated: What is the proper character of a political constitution that is itself subject to the sovereignty of the people? The point is that anyone who proposes constitutional principles makes a political claim, precisely because she or he seeks to identify the proper character of the political process and, thereby, the norms to which every political participant should explicitly adhere. Hence, a convincing democratic proposal must itself be consistent with the sovereignty of each person over her or his assessment of this very constitutional claim. Let us pose the problem by saying that a proper account of the constitution must be "self-democratizing." It should so define the political community that this very definition is subject to contestation by the citizens who are thereby defined. Unless the constitutional principles are self-democratizing in this sense, the people are not in fact finally sovereign.

Now, some may think that this condition is met if constitutional provisions include a procedure through which the people may amend or change the constitution itself. But reflection will show that this proposed solution is spurious. Because constitutional principles require all citizens to act deliberately in accord with them, many such principles would violate popular sovereignty, even if the constitution provides for its own change. To illustrate, we may consider again the necessity of religious freedom. If a given religion is declared official or established in the political community, the ethics of citizenship includes explicit adherence to it. This can only mean, as we have noted, that every citizen is constitutionally bound to accept the official conviction about ultimate worth as the basis for evaluating all political possibilities. Hence, political participation that makes a claim for or is based on some other ultimate terms of assessment is illegitimate. That the constitution also provides for its own change is inconsequential, because citizens are bound to assess even proposals for such change, like all others, in terms of the official religious conviction. Those who hold a different religious belief and seek to amend the constitution accordingly cannot act legitimately unless, absurdly, they explicitly accept the religion they in fact reject. No such provision for change, in other words, can cancel this stipulation of a political claim to all citizens, whereby popular sovereignty is violated.

This contradiction between popular sovereignty and established religion also extends to any constitutional provision that articulates a substantive principle of justice. As is well known, the Universal Declaration of Human Rights endorsed by the United Nations in 1948 includes not only political and civil but also certain economic and social rights. In this respect, the Declaration has been widely affirmed in subsequent moral and political thought. I take no exception to this affirmation. But whether all such rights should be stipulated or guaranteed in a democratic constitution is another question. Consider, for instance, a provision that all citizens have rights to productive employment or to a certain level of income or of education, whereby the state has the duty to ensure such benefits or conditions. Explicit adherence to this norm then belongs to the ethics of citizenship, and this can only mean that every citizen's political conclusions should be consistent with the prescription in question. No citizen can legitimately advocate a political purpose or policy that conflicts with the stipulated economic or social rights of all, at least if she or he is aware of the conflict. No political participant, in other words, could legitimately contest those rights. Again, the sovereignty of each citizen over her or his assessment of every political claim is violated, and any such account of the constitution fails to be self-democratizing.

A like problem marks the more abstract proposal that a constitution becomes democratic by separating the nature of justice from conceptions of the comprehensive good or understandings of the good human life overall. This view is more abstract because its central feature is said to avoid constitutional stipulation of any substantive principles of justice. The provision is only that such principles can and should be determined independently of any comprehensive good. Several recent thinkers have defended this course as the only principled way to have common decision making in a manner consistent with religious freedom. Hence, they assert, the separation they advocate has been implied by the long-standing resolve, evoked by early modern religious wars, to seek terms for political community outside the authority of any given religion, so that the people may act as one notwithstanding religious differences.

In what may be the most influential political theory of the past century, for instance, John Rawls argues that democratic justice should be conceived as "freestanding" or independent of any given "comprehensive doctrine." Principles for the basic structure of society should be acceptable to reasonable citizens whose doctrines differ, so that these principles are the content of an "overlapping consensus" (see Rawls 1996). Another version of the proposal asserts that democratic citizens should hold their conceptions of the good with "moderate scepticism" and thus should seek political principles on other grounds (see Barry, especially 168f.). Moreover, something relevantly similar is implied by those thinkers who hold that political assessments (or, at least, some of them) should be defensible on "secular grounds," even if, having met this condition, a given citizen might also base her or his claims on some or other religious conviction (see, for instance, Audi).

In spite of its appeal to many, however, this kind of democratic constitution also violates popular sovereignty. Suppose that constitutional provisions include the separation of justice, even without stipulating its principles, from ideas of the comprehensive good. Explicit adherence to or acceptance of this separation is included within the ethics of citizenship. Every citizen is constitutionally bound so to assess political claims that her or his conclusion does not depend on an understanding of the good life overall. But, then, this separation is itself a political assessment stipulated to all citizens. At least to first appearances, it is difficult to see how any member of "we the people" could affirm a comprehensive good and consistently accept that valid principles of justice are independent of it. Be that as it may, a citizen for whom this separation is invalid cannot legitimately make a claim for her or his belief or assert any other political assessment she or he takes to depend on it. Against its own intent, we can say, this account also assigns to the constitution a substantive principle, because the constitution stipulates a political claim no citizen can legitimately contest. Its more abstract character notwithstanding, the proposal is not self-democratizing.

Given the failure of substantive constitutional principles to be consistent with government by the people, one might be led to commend a constitution restricted to institutionalizing a decision-making procedure. For instance, the constitution should stipulate only the several political offices and their decision-making powers, somehow basing the selection of officials directly or indirectly on majority vote of the people and providing certain protections of minorities. Thereby, the ethics of citizenship or action in accord with the constitution is exhausted by explicit adherence to the procedures. This view, which endorses what can be called a solely procedural constitution, has also been presented by political theorists. Democracy is, they say, finally a modus vivendi, that is, common acceptance of some decision-making procedure because each individual or group finds agreement advantageous when the only alternative is to fight. Moreover, the idea of democracy as solely procedural is, I suspect, widely effective in the minds of many citizens and political leaders in the contemporary United States, even if they do not give it clear and precise formulation.

Nonetheless, this view, too, is problematic. For one thing, why should we expect citizens with substantively diverse religious commitments to accept in common the specific procedures said to be democratic? Whether any suggested decision-making procedure wins agreement will depend entirely on whether evaluations by differing individuals or groups in view of their own ultimate terms happen to concur. In fact, saying that all find some given agreement advantageous concedes that it has no basis in reason, since each determines advantage in light of her or his own purposes. The agreement is, we can say, solely strategic; that is, each finds the arrangement expedient to whatever ends she or he seeks; hence, general acceptance is merely accidental. The procedures may or may not be democratic, however that is defined, and they will be broken as soon as the ends of any individual or group counsel violation.

But the more pertinent response here is this: A solely procedural constitution also fails to be self-democratizing because it stipulates an independent procedural principle of justice. Since the ethics of citizenship is restricted to observance of the procedures, justice is defined as the outcome of them. So understood, politics exemplifies what Rawls aptly calls "pure procedural justice," whereby proper activities of the state are akin to the proper distribution of winnings and losses in a fair gambling practice, for instance, betting on a horse race. Given that fair procedures for setting odds and conducting the race are observed, the just distribution necessarily results (see Rawls 1971: 85–6). In a similar way, decision through the proper political decision-making procedure is necessarily just. It follows that other criteria political participants use to evaluate political alternatives are constitutionally defined as nonpolitical or prepolitical interests, because justice requires only the procedural aggregation of diverse claims. But, now, consider a citizen for whom justice cannot be defined independently of some nonprocedural principles; for instance, she or he might believe that a valid conception of justice can be derived only from a certain religious understanding. Since the constitution stipulates that all citizens should explicitly accept that justice is purely procedural, this citizen cannot legitimately make a claim for her or his belief.

Nor does it help to say that one is free to base one's vote on whatever nonprocedural criteria one affirms. As understood in this proposal, the right to vote does not legitimate the claim in question, because the nonprocedural criteria do not represent a prepolitical interest but, rather, an alternative principle of justice. This citizen believes, in other words, that common action solely through voting is not a valid or just constitution of the political community. Saying that one may vote one's conscience is rather like saying that a gambler is free to bet based on some alternative procedure for the distribution of winnings and losses or that a socialist is free to consult her or his principles as she or he spends money in the capitalist market. A solely procedural constitution defines any nonprocedural criteria citizens affirm as matters of mere personal decision or preference, in distinction from differences about valid principles of justice. Hence, exercising one's right to vote can only endorse this stipulation rather than contest it. In its own way, then, this account also separates the nature of justice from other values – not only from conceptions of the comprehensive good but also from any nonprocedural criteria. We can even say that a solely procedural constitution is, in its own way, substantive, because the stipulation that no other criteria are required to effect justice is itself a substantive political assessment.

III THE UNION OF "WE THE PEOPLE"

We have now reviewed several attempts to state the proper character of a democratic constitution and, thereby, to define how "we the people" act as one. If the critical reflections are sound, all of these proposals are unsuccessful because each fails to be self-democratizing, that is, fails to affirm fully the right of each citizen to contest the constitution itself. In each case, including a solely procedural constitution, the defect results from placing in the proposed constitution a substantive principle of justice, adherence to which belongs to the ethics of citizenship and contestation of which is, therefore, illegitimate. Any such constitution, we may also say, violates religious freedom, which legitimates any belief about the ultimate ground of worth. This principle is the summary provision that democratic citizens are sovereign over their assessments of every political claim, so that any constitutional stipulation citizens cannot legitimately contest is inconsistent with government by the people.

Review of these several proposals may seem only to confirm the suspicion that political unity consistent with popular sovereignty is finally impossible. Clearly, the political process cannot be constituted without stipulating some or other principles, but these must somehow legitimate the sovereign assessment of themselves by each citizen so constituted. Since the principles are, by definition, those to which all citizens should explicitly adhere, how could any account of a democratic constitution be consistent with a citizen's contestation of it and thus be self-democratizing? Government by the people seems to be, like rule by anarchy, a contradiction in terms.

But we should not rush to that judgment. Another alternative is, I believe, available, and appreciation of it will allow us to pursue with greater precision whether and, if so, why the Christian faith affirms in our time and place a democratic political community. We can approach this alternative through further reflection on the right of every citizen to make or contest any political claim. In order to begin on this course, I propose to appropriate from two German thinkers, Jürgen Habermas and Karl-Otto Apel, the following proposition: Making a political claim, including one that contests another claim, is a communicative act in which one pledges to any recipient that one's claim can be validated or redeemed by argument and, therefore, also concedes that one's claim may be invalidated in the same way (see Habermas 1990: 43–115; Apel). This statement, I recognize, might itself be contested, and I will return shortly to that possibility. For the moment, however, let us assume this understanding of political claims. Having done so, we can now infer that the one common commitment consistent with any political disagreement is the readiness to have conflicting claims assessed by argument. In other words, participation in the practice of political argumentation is the one activity that is explicitly neutral to or does not explicitly takes sides in any possible political disagreement.

Given this accounting, the way is open for a self-democratizing constitution. Constitutional principles have this character if they define the political association as a full and free political discussion and debate or a full and free political discourse. To insist that the discourse is full means that no political claim is immune from contestation and, if contested, is open to debate. Thereby, the principle of religious freedom is reaffirmed, since no belief about the ultimate terms of political assessment can be official or beyond debate. To insist that the discourse is free means that all members of the political community are equal participants, at liberty to advocate or contest any political claim. Thereby, the sovereignty of each over her or his assessment of every such claim is reaffirmed. This sovereignty is consistent with action-as-one because all affirm that claims for ultimate terms of political assessment can be validated or invalidated by argument and, therefore, activities of the state are properly determined only by claims argument can redeem.[6] The people are the final authority because they rule together as equals through full and free political discourse.

A democratic constitution, then, should stipulate no more and no less than (a) the rights that define all citizens as always potential and sometimes actual participants in political argumentation and (b) the decision-making procedures or set of institutions and offices through which political discourse determines the state's activities.[7] Defining politics as a full and free discourse differentiates this constitution from all that include a substantive principle, and, accordingly, the ethics

---

6. Strictly speaking, then, a claim is not properly political unless, among other things, it can be validated or invalidated through discourse. To claim justice for some actual or proposed activity of the state on the basis of understandings discourse cannot assess is to deny that ultimate terms of assessment can be established by argument.

7. This does not imply that democratic discourse properly occurs only within formal institutions of political rule, such as legislatures, courts, policy-making bodies more or less directly related to the government, and political caucuses and campaigns. To the contrary, political discourse is present wherever members of "we the people" make political claims, so that the media, civic associations, educational institutions, and virtually any other kind of interaction can be contexts encompassed by the democratic process through which influence on the determination of state activities occurs.

of citizenship consists in no more and no less than commitment to political rule through this argumentative practice.

So understood, I will call the constitutional principles "formative" principles of justice, in distinction from "substantive" principles that do not properly constitute but, rather, are objects of the discussion and debate through which the people govern themselves. The mark of a formative principle is this: Action in accord with it is explicitly neutral to any possible political disagreement because the principle prescribes nothing other than participation in a practice of political discourse about contested claims. In contrast, action in accord with a substantive principle of justice is explicitly partisan or takes sides in some or other political disagreement. Consider, for instance, a principle of economic rights that requires governmentally guaranteed employment or a guaranteed annual income; action in accord with this principle is partisan in a disagreement with someone for whom the government should be minimal, limited to defending the nation, preventing crime, enforcing contracts, and the like. In contrast, the principle of religious freedom is formative. Because it stipulates the right of every citizen to decide for herself or himself the ultimate terms of political assessment, the action prescribed is simply respect for the sovereignty of all citizens over every political claim and thus is explicitly neutral to any possible political disagreement.

Roughly speaking, formative and substantive principles differ in the way that Robert's Rules of Order are distinguished from the business of a meeting conducted in accord with them. Just as those rules would have no point were there no meetings, we should note, democracy as constituted by formative principles makes no sense unless some substantive principle or principles of justice are valid. Government through full and free discussion and debate is impossible without something to argue about. A formative constitution presupposes, therefore, that principles by which proper political purposes are determined can be redeemed in discourse. Formative principles, we can say, stipulate *that* there is some valid substantive principle or principles, and the people are morally bound to rule in accord with ultimate terms of political assessment open to validation by argument. But it is no business of a democratic constitution to stipulate *what* those substantive principles or ultimate terms of political assessment are, explicit address to that question being left entirely to the constituted discussion and debate. If we read the Preamble

46

to the United States Constitution as formative in character, it states no substantive principle in declaring the framework ordained and established "to form a more perfect union, establish justice, insure domestic tranquility, provide for the common defense, promote the general welfare, and secure the blessings of liberty." On this reading, the Preamble stipulates only that there are valid understandings of "a more perfect union," "justice," "domestic tranquility," and the rest, so that what those understandings are and how they should be specified in activities of the state are precisely what the people as the final authority determine through discussion and debate.

Naturally, the political process as it reaches decision legislates substantive norms or activities of the state and asserts them as substantively right or good. The people may decide to prohibit certain restraints of trade, control the possession of guns, protect the environment in specific ways, provide public education, subsidize housing for the poor, and so forth. But these are statutory outcomes rather than constitutional provisions. While all legislation enjoins all members of the political community to act accordingly, statutory decisions do not prescribe, as the constitution does, assessments to which citizens must explicitly adhere *as participants in political discourse*. Thus, every citizen remains sovereign over her or his own assessment of legislated norms or policies, meaning that she or he is free to contest them and advocate repeal or change through the democratic political process.

It then follows that statutory enactments can never include any prescription that explicitly requires citizens as political participants to affirm certain substantive principles or norms. The state violates its democratic character if legislation stipulates the terms in which governing directives should be assessed. For instance, the legislature cannot prescribe that the public schools should teach or favor in their teaching a certain religion, since doing so asserts terms for all assessments and thus for the political assessments of citizens. This is why religious freedom means not only the absence of an official religion provided by the constitution but also the prohibition of any law that establishes religion.

To all that has been said, however, some may object that a formative constitution still stipulates too much. It, too, can only be inconsistent with popular sovereignty because no constitution can avoid stipulating principles of political union. Let us assume, without pausing to offer specific argument, that the rights defining each person as a potential and sometimes actual participant in political discourse include rights to life, bodily integrity, and personal property and, further, certain specifically political rights, such as those to free speech, assembly, and equal protection of the laws. A constitution that provides these rights stipulates principles to which all members of the political community should explicitly adhere and, according to the objection, thereby makes political claims that cannot be legitimately contested. This objection, I believe, can be turned aside. If constitutional principles are truly formative or necessary to a full and free political discourse, action in accord with them is explicitly neutral even to dissent from them. This follows because the action prescribed is nothing other than participation in the practice of argumentation about contested political claims, and that action is explicitly neutral even to disagreement about the formative principles themselves. To dissent from such principles or from democracy itself is to issue the pledge that one's dissent can be redeemed by argument. Thus, honoring the rights of every person as a member of "we the people" is explicitly neutral even to a disagreement about these rights. So far as I can see, a constitution in accord with which the people act together through full and free discourse is itself consistent with the sovereignty of each citizen over her or his assessment of that very constitution. It is self-democratizing.[8]

IV DEMOCRACY AND THE WAY OF REASON

Democracy conceived as rule by way of unrestricted argument is thoroughly dependent on the basic cultural change we reviewed earlier. In contrast to medieval civilization, the modern age increasingly affirmed reason as alone sufficient to validate understandings of reality and the human good and thus increasingly denied the need

---

8. I recognize that some will object to a solely formative constitution because it stipulates too little. On this objection, the right to participate in full and free political discourse is hollow or worthless in the absence of rights to certain economic and social conditions, for instance, to a certain level of economic security and an opportunity for education. Hence, a solely formative constitution is at odds with itself, calling for a political process whose necessary conditions it does not fully provide. I will take up this objection in Chapter 4, whose discussion provides a more complete context in which to consider the relation of formative and substantive principles of justice (see Chapter 4, Section II).

for religious authority to determine principles of belief and practice. The Enlightenment gave this change culminating expression. Naturally, the Enlightenment was a complex period or movement, and many convictions were or are associated with it. With respect to the present point, however, the only important feature is the commitment to reason as alone sufficient to validate understandings. Alfred North Whitehead's summary is elegant: "The appeal to history [that is, to the insight of our predecessors] is the appeal to summits of attainment beyond any immediate clarity in our own individual existence. It is an appeal to authority. The appeal to reason is the appeal to that ultimate judge, universal and yet individual to each, to which all authority must bow. History has authority so far, and exactly so far, as it admits of some measure of rational interpretation" (Whitehead 1961: 162). I will call this the "humanistic commitment" and define it as follows: Our understandings of reality and ourselves can be validated or redeemed only through reasons authorized finally by our common human experience. If government by the people must be constituted as a full and free discourse, popular sovereignty is, we may say, the political form of this humanistic commitment.

Something very similar to this commitment was shared by some of those principally responsible for conceiving the United States Constitution and, specifically, the principle of religious freedom articulated in the First Amendment. As heirs to cultural developments in modern Europe, men such as Benjamin Franklin, Thomas Jefferson, and James Madison were children of the Enlightenment who "concluded that reform depended upon the freeing of man's natural reason from . . . enslavement – largely by opening all the channels of communication through freedom of speech, freedom of the press, freedom to assemble and petition, so that every opinion could have a hearing" (Mead: 46). In his "Notes on the State of Virginia," Jefferson wrote that "reason and free inquiry are the only effectual agents against error. Give a loose to them, they will support the true religion by bringing every false one to their tribunal" (Jefferson: 394). He gave the same view unsurpassed statement in defending his Act for Establishing Religious Freedom in Virginia: "Truth is great and will prevail if left to herself; . . . she is the proper and sufficient antagonist to error, and has nothing to fear from the conflict [among religions] unless by human interposition disarmed of her natural weapons, free argument and debate; errors ceasing to be dangerous when it is permitted freely to contradict them" (Jefferson: 391).

I do not deny that the United States Constitution and its First Amendment were the product of a complicated historical process and were shaped in part by divergent interests somehow taken into account, most especially the southern interest in protecting slavery. "Great ideas," Whitehead also wrote, "enter into reality with evil associates and with disgusting alliances" (Whitehead 1961: 18). In addition, opinions about how best to understand the new republic's design were at the time, as they have been throughout the nation's subsequent history, diverse. Accordingly, I have no wish to argue that the idea or ideal of a full and free political discourse was the controlling influence on the Constitution or that this constitution, even with subsequent amendments, adequately exemplifies that ideal. My main concern is with defensible democratic principles, and I seek to show that rule through full and free argument is the only coherent meaning of government by the people. Still, the apparent fact that some leading founders of the American republic self-consciously shared the Enlightenment's affirmation of reason supports the judgment, expressed earlier, that the meaning of democracy reached eminent expression in their minds.

If the humanistic commitment was historically important to modern democracy, we can also state this connection another way: Commitment to the way of reason, as we may call it, entails the denial of any principled grounds for political inequality. Perhaps the conditions of Aquinas's context justified his belief in rule by one or the few. But the assertion of natural human inequality essential to his account is contradicted by the affirmation that reason alone is sufficient to validate claims about reality and human good. Once this affirmation is accepted, there is no theoretical way to stop the drive to popular sovereignty. Any attempt to arrest it must grant political privilege to certain claims because of who makes them. For instance, claims made by persons of wealth or supposed virtue or special circumstances of birth or a certain religious community must be given superior rights in determination of the state's activities. But the way of reason does not privilege persons, that is, does not credit claims based on who makes them. The sole criterion is whether claims can be redeemed in discourse. The logic of the way of reason is political discourse inclusive of all.

Conversely, no attempt to defend political equality without the humanistic commitment can be fully adequate. If, for instance, one derives democracy from a given religious belief, even while this belief is itself immune to discursive validation, one stipulates a fundamental principle of equality that finally can only be asserted. I do not mean that contemporary religious beliefs cannot have their own substantive grounds for rejecting medieval views of natural stratification. But any grounds for political equality that exclude the way of reason are finally self-refuting. They imply that principles of justice themselves depend on something argument cannot redeem, thereby denying to citizens who reject those grounds an equal right to participate in political rule. Otherwise stated, ultimate terms for politics exclusive of the humanistic commitment imply, in the sense mentioned earlier, privileged persons, namely, those who affirm those ultimate terms, and thus full political equality is arrested. This simply repeats that popular sovereignty makes sense only as government through full and free discourse. Whatever else is involved in the modern emergence of democracy, we cannot consistently endorse it if its reversal of the Western political tradition is separated from its embrace of the way of reason.

But if this is correct, then we have clarified the commitment Christian faith must allow its adherents if they are consistently to affirm democratic equality. The question we must now answer is whether Christians may consistently affirm politics through full and free discourse, which means submitting their own belief about ultimate worth, like any other, to validation or invalidation by argument. Absent a positive answer, Christian faith cannot endorse government by the people and, with it, politics as a common Christian vocation.

Having arrived at this conclusion, we are also bound to recognize that, for many Christians, it renders the relation of Christian faith and democratic politics problematic. For them, belief in God as all-embracing love, whom humans are called to love without reservation, cannot be validated without appeal to God's self-disclosure through Jesus Christ. Thus, Christian faith cannot be redeemed or, at least, fully redeemed by argument. Moreover, this belief about Christian faith is itself taken to be a part of Christian faith; that is, the incompetence of reason to know fully the nature of God is itself known only by way of God's revelation through Jesus Christ. Whether these Christians appropriately represent the content of Christian faith will be discussed in the next chapter. But the very fact that they so believe occasions a question about the understanding of democracy developed here and requires a return to an important issue waived earlier.

My account of popular sovereignty assumed that making a political claim, including a claim for some ultimate terms of political assessment, is a communicative act in which one pledges that one's claim can be redeemed by argument. Before proceeding from this assumption, I noted that it, too, might be contested. If applied to religious claims, it is one many political thinkers, whether or not they consider themselves religious, do indeed deny. They hold that differences among "comprehensive doctrines" or conceptions of the good cannot be validated or invalidated by the way of reason, and thus they do not agree that making a religious claim affirms argumentative assessment. This leads some to seek the separation of justice from all such doctrines or conceptions. The dissent is shared even by Habermas and Apel, from whom the proposition about political claims was borrowed. On their view, someone who declares a belief about the comprehensive good does not make a genuine claim to validity at all, or at least not a political one.[9]

But the central point here is that many Christians join, in their own way, the protest against assessing religious claims by discourse – as do many other religious believers. For these citizens, the ultimate terms of political assessment transcend reason or argumentative validation. The apparent consequence for democracy is this: Constituting politics as an argumentative practice is not self-democratizing. If the constitution prescribes discourse about conflicting religious convictions, the ethics of citizenship includes explicit adherence to this prescription, and thereby the political community fails to legitimate the belief of those for whom ultimate terms of assessment are not open to discursive validation. Hence, the sovereignty of such religious believers over their assessment of the constitution is denied.

Indeed, some might advance this objection notwithstanding that they themselves share the humanistic commitment. Even if religious

9. Habermas's view appears to be somewhat more complicated. He holds that convictions about the good life are pertinent to the politics of a given democratic community as it seeks to determine an "authentic collective self-understanding." But every such conviction is dependent in all respects on the specific lifeworld shared by individuals in that community and, in that sense, on shared premises that cannot themselves be redeemed through discourse (1996: 108; see chap. 7).

claims can be argumentatively assessed, this form of the objection contends, some religious adherents believe to the contrary; thus, constituting politics by the way of reason stipulates a political claim these citizens cannot legitimately contest. It will be useful to examine the objection in this form, because its conclusion is, I believe, inconsistent with its concession. If the religious question *is* a rational one, meaning that answers to it can be rationally assessed, then, as I will argue, constitution of a full and free discourse in fact legitimates even a denial of the way of reason. Should this argument be successful, the only real issue for Christians or anyone else will be whether religious convictions can, in truth, be validated and invalidated by argument.

Grant for the moment that the religious question defines a rational order of reflection; that is, differing beliefs in answer to this question can, in truth, be validated and invalidated by arguments that do not assume the truth of one or another answer.[10] Now consider a religion whose answer includes the belief that this very answer transcends reason, because, say, this answer can be validated only by appeal to God's special revelation. It follows that this religion, inclusive of its assertion about the need for God's special self-disclosure, is, in truth, an answer to a rational question. In spite of what the religion asserts, then, its answer can be validated or invalidated by argument. If this is so, those who claim truth for this answer thereby pledge that their religious conviction can be assessed by appeal to reason, even if they do not concede the point. Someone who makes this claim is similar

10. In speaking here and subsequently of whether the religious question is rational, I use "religious" to designate the meaning of an explicit belief about the ultimate ground of worth and human existence in relation to it in the sense that the belief claims to be valid for all humans. The issue, then, is whether a religious claim in this sense can be validated or invalidated by discourse. I note this because one might speak of the religious question in another sense. In this work, I include within the class of religious beliefs all explicit convictions about ultimate worth, because these are, on my accounting, the beliefs protected by the principle of religious freedom. Strictly speaking, however, I understand the class of religious beliefs to include only some of the beliefs embraced by religious freedom, because the distinctive function of religious activity is to mediate an explicit belief about ultimate worth as we humans lead our lives, that is, to cultivate a life determined or informed by that belief. Hence, someone who asks the religious question is concerned to know not only what belief about ultimate worth is universally valid but also what representations or practices mediate this belief, and an answer to the religious question in the latter sense may or may not claim to be valid for all humans. I will not pursue whether the religious question in this latter sense is, in its own way, rational – although I think that the answer is affirmative. My concern is the relation between religious and political claims and, accordingly, whether religious claims are rational in the sense that they claim to be valid for all who do or might participate in political discourse.

in a relevant way to someone who makes a promise. The act of promising is a commitment to do what is promised, whatever the content of the promise may be. If the religious question is rational, the claim made for any answer to it, regardless of content, endorses argumentative assessment. Thus, democracy as a full and free political discourse legitimates even religious dissent from the prescription that religious differences be adjudicated by discourse. This dissent occasions a political disagreement to which the practice of argumentation is, in truth, explicitly neutral, and those whose religion leads them to contest the way of reason are invited as members of "we the people" to argue for the limits to reason they assert.

To be sure, if the religious question is rational, then "I hereby claim validity for religious belief *X*, which reason does not have the capacity to assess" is similar to "I hereby promise to do *Y*, which I do not have the capacity to do." Just as the act of promising implies that one cannot sensibly promise something beyond one's powers, so the act of claiming validity implies that a religious belief whose validation is beyond reason cannot be valid. Thus, a formative constitution, because it explicitly affirms the possibility of religious discourse, more or less obviously *implies* that claims for the suprarational character of religious truth are invalid. But the self-democratizing character required of a constitution cannot mean its implicit consistency with every possible religious belief or every possible political assessment one or another sovereign citizen might assert, since these beliefs and assessments will be, at least in all likelihood, inconsistent with each other. In order to ensure popular sovereignty, the constitution must be *explicitly* neutral to every possible political disagreement. What government by the people requires is the equal importance of each person's sovereign assessment, the constitutional stipulation that every such assessment is equally legitimate. If the religious question is rational, precisely such equal importance is given by giving each citizen equal standing in the political discourse. A full and free political discourse, we may repeat, is explicitly neutral to or legitimates all political claims because it prescribes only what is pledged by any political claim, whatever its content.[11]

---

11. In technical terms, we can say that formative principles of a democratic constitution derive solely from the *pragmatic* character of political claims to validity, in distinction from the *semantic* or propositional content for which validity is claimed. Hence, the semantic content of a claim may or may not agree with the principles

IV. Democracy and the Way of Reason

Taking this argument to be sound, we can reach the real issue. Politics by the way of reason itself violates religious freedom only if the religious question is *not* a rational one, that is, only if those for whom religious truth is suprarational are right. On that assumption, a formative constitution fails to legitimate dissent from what the constitution stipulates, and it fails to be self-democratizing. But, then, no constitution can be truly democratic – at least if the criticisms advanced earlier against alternative proposals are convincing. So far as I can see, to assume that ultimate terms for political assessment transcend reason is to imply that government by the people cannot be coherently understood. Hence, the cost of denying politics by the way of discourse is the impossibility of democracy. The relation between Christian faith and the way of reason is, therefore, the next subject to be addressed.

to which the pragmatic character of making the claim commits a political participant. If the religious question defines a rational order of reflection, a person who claims validity for a religious belief purporting to be beyond reason contradicts the semantic content of her or his claim in the pragmatic act of making it.

Chapter 3

Faith and the Way of Reason

Does Christian faith affirm the principles of democratic politics? In the contemporary United States, a relatively few Christians might answer "no," perhaps because they believe that Christian faith prescribes a withdrawal from the concerns of this world or, more specifically, from politics. But most, I expect, would readily answer "yes." Thereby, they would stand with most Christians in United States history, for whom their faith has supplied the deepest reason to uphold the democratic ideals of this republic. In recent history, no American gave more eloquent or profound expression to the harmony between God's purpose and those ideals than did Martin Luther King, Jr., through whose incisive cadences the movement for equality in the mid-twentieth century appealed simultaneously to the divine calling and the American creed. But however easily most Christians may embrace democracy, their doing so with integrity depends on accepting a relation between faith and reason they may not so readily affirm. The argument here for politics as a common Christian vocation also depends on that relation. This calling, I seek to show, belongs to Christians generally because Christian faith prescribes democracy. Hence, we must now ask whether Christian faith is consistent with the way of reason.

I DEFINING THE QUESTION

Government by the people, the previous chapter concluded, gives political form to the humanistic commitment, so that the former cannot be consistently endorsed without the latter. Democracy requires that religious convictions can be validated or invalidated in the argumentative practice of "we the people." The democratic way, we can also say, includes religious freedom. To be sure, most American Christians would also accept this principle as one that presents no conflict with their faith. But religious freedom means that every member of the political community is sovereign over her or his belief about the ultimate terms of political assessment, so that action-as-one has a basis in principle only if all citizens can be united through full and free discourse. In sum, democracy presupposes that the religious question is a rational one.

The contemporary importance of this conclusion is marked by the widespread doubt that religious claims can be assessed in discourse. At least within the Western world, probably most men and women take religious beliefs to be or to depend on perspectives beyond the reach of unbiased reasoning. In some form or other, a similar view widely characterizes theoretical discussion. If this view is correct, the virtually unanimous commitment to democratic politics cannot affirm popular sovereignty without incoherence, and something seems basically amiss in modern Western civilization. This consequence, I hope, will counsel those for whom religious convictions transcend rational validation and invalidation to reconsider their accounting. Be that as it may, taking note of how pervasive their accounting is at least helps to identify one part of our concern about faith and reason. How this relation should be understood depends in part on whether the humanistic commitment makes sense. Neither Christians nor anyone else can sensibly affirm discourse about religious claims if, in truth, religious beliefs cannot be validated and invalidated in this way. Hence, our current discussion includes the question: Does the way of reason make sense?

In spite of how demanding many take this issue to be, I will not give it extended attention here. Instead, I will henceforth presuppose that assessment of religious convictions by the way of reason is indeed possible. Perhaps taking this course will seem to resolve by mere supposition some complicated disputes about a fundamental problem. But I cannot see how anyone who critically questions the humanistic commitment can avoid presupposing it. To ask critically whether religious claims can be assessed through discourse is to seek argument for a positive or negative answer. But a negative answer, so far as I can see, cannot be successfully defended by argument, because reason cannot establish that religious truth is suprarational. One can only assert that this view of religious truth also transcends what discourse can assess – and thereby withdraw from the debate. In contrast, there is a way to defeat that view or to defend the positive answer, namely, by giving a sound argument for a given religious conviction.[1] Hence, raising the question critically commits one to the positive answer. Posing the issue for debate, we might say, is similar to asking someone to decide whether she or he has the power of decision; doing so presupposes that the power is present, and those who think otherwise can only refuse to put the question. Asking for reasons to affirm or deny the way of reason presupposes its credibility.[2]

Nonetheless, these brief comments will hardly settle the issue for those contemporary Christians persuaded that their affirmation of faith transcends the limits of reason. They will and, perhaps, should be given substantial pause about politics by way of full and free discourse unless Christian faith allows them to affirm the argumentative assessment of their belief in God as revealed through Jesus Christ. Even if the way of reason is possible, in other words, it remains that democratic politics cannot make sense as a Christian vocation unless Christian faith itself is consistent with the humanistic commitment. I take this to be the fundamental issue for our discussion, especially pressing because contemporary Christians are prominent within the pervasive Western consensus that denies rational validation and invalidation of religious claims.

In this denial, moreover, Christians today can claim continuity with most of the Christian tradition. Clearly, the history of Christian thought has not spoken with one voice about the place of reason within the life of Christian faith and, specifically, whether reason can establish that God has truly been revealed through Jesus Christ. The issues were summarily formulated by Tertullian during the second century of the Common Era in his now famous question: "What has Jerusalem to do with Athens?" Tertullian himself minimized such

---

1. To be sure, one might argue that no religious beliefs can be validated because, as claims to truth, all such beliefs are confused, that is, the religious question itself is nonsensical. I suspect that those who so assert often use "religion" in a more narrow sense than I intend in this work. Be that as it may, any who so argue are already committed to the way of reason.
2. The Appendix offers a more extended argument for this presupposition, although the discussion there is based in part on conclusions that will be defended subsequently in this chapter.

doing, but he thereby advanced only one among many positions in a tradition profoundly contentious about how faith relates to reason. For present purposes, however, we need not review the various answers that have been proposed. Whether reason is assigned a minimal or substantially more important task, the Christian tradition transmits an overwhelming consensus that true belief about God and human salvation cannot be fully validated independently of God's self-disclosure through Jesus Christ and the scriptural witness to it – and this consensus includes Augustine and Aquinas, as well as Luther and Calvin. I will call it the "majority voice" of the Christian tradition. If democracy presupposes the way of reason, then a Christian embrace of popular sovereignty requires a basis in Christian faith for departing from this majority voice.

The issue may also be formulated this way: Does Christian faith distinguish between its own meaning, on the one hand, and its validity, on the other? I have in mind here the commonplace distinction we all employ when, for instance, we understand what someone means in speaking as she or he does but we are not sure whether what she or he says is true. If Christian faith authorizes the humanistic commitment, it thereby implies a difference between the understanding of ultimate worth Christians *claim to be true*, on the one hand, and, on the other, whether that understanding *is true*. What Christians claim to be true is, as mentioned earlier, determined by the primary norm for understanding God and human existence as revealed through Jesus Christ. Whether any understanding so authorized is true depends on whether it can be validated through reasons authorized by common human experience. As I will emphasize in a moment, the point is not that Christians should always live with doubt about their own belief; to the contrary, they cannot witness to their faith without affirming it. Still, the distinction is required because a claim for Christian faith carries the pledge that it can be, if it becomes problematic or is contested, validated by argument and, therefore, the concession that it may be invalidated in the same way. Commitment to discourse entails that no religious understanding or conviction can be valid simply because some institution or some tradition claims truth for it. Thereby, such commitment implies a difference between what the understanding means and whether it is valid.

To avoid a misreading, we should also clarify what this distinction does not say. Assent to it does not deny that Christian witness equates the truth about ultimate worth with the meaning of Christian faith. In stressing this undeniable fact, one simply insists that Christians claim validity for their faith. To act on the Christian understanding of reality and human life is explicitly or implicitly to assert that ultimate worth is truly what Christian faith takes it to be. But if Christians rightly affirm the discursive validation and invalidation of their claim, then their every witness implies the difference between what Christian faith means and whether it is true.

At the same time, affirming or implying this difference does not say that argumentative assessment of religious claims is a simple process or that agreement on its conclusions is easily reached. With respect to most important matters, disagreements within the human community do not easily yield to reasoned reflection, even when we make our best efforts to pursue the truth free from the interference of other interests. Both in discourse with each other and in our private dialogues with ourselves, the most we can hope for in most situations is progress toward rather than arrival at something like complete resolution, and the conclusions we reach are always open to subsequent doubt and reconsideration based on evidence and argument we did not previously entertain or appreciate. When the claims at issue are religious and, therefore, concern the most fundamental questions about reality and human life, the way of reason exacts a recognition that the difficulties may be equally profound. For these reasons, democracy requires that no activity of the state may compromise the constitutionally stipulated conditions of a full and free discourse. Thereby, the discussion and debate about the state's activities and, as a part of this, about the ultimate terms of political assessment never ends, and decisions that have been taken can be reassessed and possibly reversed. Thus, to ask if Christians should distinguish the meaning of their faith from its validity is to raise a question of principle. The issue is not whether assessment by argument is an easy process but, instead, whether commitment to it is consistent with Christian faith.

II THE MAJORITY VOICE

We mentioned that Christians today cannot endorse the way of reason without a departure from most of their tradition. Whatever differences on the relation between faith and reason Christian history includes, its majority voice has said that a true understanding of God and human salvation cannot be fully validated without appeal to God's self-disclosure through Jesus Christ. In this sense, the dominant tradition has set limits to reason. Given that democracy is a possible form of political community, an assertion of such limits cannot be true, because full and free political discourse is impossible unless religious claims can be argumentatively assessed. But the democratic ideal does not itself determine whether contemporary Christians may depart from the majority voice of their tradition. The answer to that question depends on the meaning of their faith.

We can approach this answer by seeing the similarity between this departure and another we pursued earlier. Our concern with politics as a Christian vocation turned to the proper character of democracy because the emergence of political communities that are or approach being democratic may give contemporary Christians reason to depart from the early account. To be sure, we are still in the process of discussing this possibility because we have not yet established that Christian faith affirms popular sovereignty. But if our altered circumstances do make a difference to the political responsibilities of Christians, then something about the abiding content of Christian faith will follow, namely, that it does not include the view of political responsibility apparently present in Paul and given comprehensive statement by Augustine, at least on one reading of him. In like manner, the present question concerns whether the majority voice in Christian history expresses the abiding content of Christian faith and is, therefore, authoritative for contemporary Christians.

A departure from the early account might, I argued, still honor those who framed it, in the sense that its political prescriptions were fitting applications of Christian faith to the specific circumstances of the time, namely, a situation in which rule by the many was not possible. Moreover, that reading of Paul or Augustine does not require that they took their understanding of political responsibility to depend on their specific situation. Perhaps recognition of this dependence could itself be expected only given later and differing conditions because, for instance, circumstances in which the early account would not be applicable were at the time unforeseeable. The difference between abiding content and its specification to variable circumstances does not imply that clarity about what belongs to the one and what to the other must itself be abiding. To the contrary, explications of the difference themselves depend on the variable circumstances of time and place. In the nature of the case, every formulation of Christian self-understanding, however creative it may be, is conditioned not only by inherited institutional patterns but also by specific cultural and conceptual resources available in its historical context.

This last point is especially important to our present concern. The majority voice, which has denied to reason full validation of Christian belief, has also typically asserted that this understanding of reason's limits belongs to the abiding content of Christian faith. Indeed, the assertion seems virtually inseparable from the denial. A concession that changed circumstances might permit assessment of Christian faith by argument would seem to imply that it *can* be so assessed, even if one is not immediately clear how to realize the possibility. Be that as it may, the majority voice has in fact taken its account to be essential to the meaning of Christian faith. But if a statement of what does and does not belong to this abiding content may itself depend on the available cultural or conceptual resources, then the majority voice may still not be authoritative for contemporary Christians.

A departure from it appears more plausible than it otherwise might when we recall that popular sovereignty emerged against a larger background of cultural changes, the most basic of which was increasingly widespread commitment to reason as alone sufficient to validate understandings of reality and the human good. Insofar as the cultural sweep of this affirmation is especially distinctive to modernity's later expressions, there are grounds to suppose that the cultural and conceptual resources with which Christian self-understanding might now be explicated have altered. Perhaps they permit a recognition not so readily available to earlier statements of Christian self-understanding, namely, that the limits to reason asserted by the majority voice are not essential to Christian belief.

If this recognition is an appropriate expression of Christian faith in our time and, further, is more readily available within emergent modern conditions, then contemporary Christians may not need to fault Augustine or Aquinas or, more generally, earlier Christians for whom differing cultural circumstances conditioned a different account. The majority voice is now said to be mistaken, but this conclusion has the advantage of later circumstances and need not entail the further judgment that all those who contributed to the dominant tradition were insofar without justification. Given the cultural circumstances and conceptual resources in terms of which they formulated Christian self-understanding, one might judge, it is presumptuous to censure their belief about reason's limits. In this respect, the majority voice might be similar to the early account, insofar as the latter was thought to belong to the abiding content of Christian faith.

On that reading, both cases confirm an important general fact: Fidelity to the community that for centuries has confessed Jesus as the Christ does not require contemporary Christian assent to inherited formulations of Christian faith. Indeed, such assent is impossible, since Christians in the past disagreed with each other. Nonetheless, Christians today have their confession only with indebtedness to their tradition. Critical revision of its dominant explications becomes a betrayal of this integral dependence unless an explanation can be given for why the faith was expressed in ways contemporary Christians should not repeat. Thus, a departure in favor of the humanistic commitment cannot be completely convincing unless the specific conditions conducive to the majority voice can be identified, in a manner similar to showing that the early account could be asserted with the force of abiding authority because government as rule by the many was not a realistic anticipation. At the same time, however, an effort to meet this demand would require the kind of extended historical inquiry that would alter in a major way the character of this work. In lieu of that inquiry, I will illustrate the relevant kind of accounting by brief attention to the philosophical context in which earlier explications of Christian belief occurred. This discussion, then, does not pretend to be an adequate explanation but, rather, seeks only to suggest certain aspects of the cultural context that may have been important conditions shaping the majority voice.

According to the historian of philosophy Pierre Hadot, we misunderstand the Greco-Roman world in which early Christianity appeared if we see the practice of philosophy as essentially similar to the academic pursuit typically found in modern universities. To the contrary, philosophy was a "way of life," in or through which those committed to it sought to become fully human or to attain the highest form of human existence (see Hadot). While the practice clearly included reasoned discourse about the nature of the cosmos, human behavior, and reason itself, the "love of wisdom" was not a pursuit of abstract discourse for its own sake. The wisdom one loved was, rather, an existential orientation or complete way of life in accord with the laws of reason or rational nature of things. To be a philosopher was to participate in one or another "school" or tradition of practice, most of which originated in the Greek context prior to the Common Era – Platonic, Aristotelian, Stoic, Epicurean, Skeptic. Each of these involved fundamental conceptions of the world and continuing arguments about them, but both were inseparable from "spiritual exercises," certain disciplines of thought, mental attention, and behavior through which life oriented by those conceptions was cultivated. Thus, we should distinguish, as the Stoics in fact did, "between *discourse about* philosophy and *philosophy itself*" (Hadot: 266), the latter being precisely the way of life to which philosophical theories were but servants.

Assuming that Hadot's broad point, as I have stated it, is substantially correct, we can say that early Christians understood their faith to be an existential alternative to the philosophical orientations of Hellenistic culture.[3] As a consequence, early attempts to relate Christian faith and philosophy were finally addressed to explicating the similarities and differences between ways of life. Whatever similarities obtained, one summary difference worth noting is this: Philosophy was typically understood as an alternative reserved for a minority because "philosophy itself" required that one be able to practice "discourse about philosophy," that is, to engage in theoretical reflection or argumentation. In contrast, Christian faith was widely proclaimed to be a possibility available to people generally. Behind this contrast was a more fundamental difference: For Christians, existential authenticity was not something achieved through practices or disciplines open only to the few because the decisive action was God's own, offering salvation humans cannot give to themselves and need only accept. In this sense, early Christian thinkers had good grounds to distinguish the way of faith from the life of reason. Because the reasoning essential to philosophical practices included discourse about ultimate matters, perhaps marking the difference also led some

3. "An entire current of ancient Christian thought," Hadot continues, "defined Christianity itself as a philosophy," although, he also emphasizes, "there can be no question of denying the incomparable originality of Christianity" and thus "the specifically Christian character of this 'philosophy'" (Hadot: 127, 129). But my limited purpose here does not require engagement with the sophistication of Hadot's account. The current paragraph, then, uses "philosophy" to mean a way of life different from the way of Christian faith.

Christians to deny that reason could fully determine the truth about human existence and its divine source and end.

Insofar as this interpretation has merit, the early encounter of Christian faith and philosophy has left an enduring mark on Christian assessments of reason. One recurring defense of limits to reason betrays the assumption that differing ways of life are in question. On this formulation, failure to place Christian belief beyond argumentative validation implies that humans can bring themselves and others to existential authenticity through the exercise of reasoned discourse; thereby, one denies that salvation is by God's grace alone, received through faith. So far as I can see, however, this account involves a confusion. To hold that argument can validate Christian belief in God's prior act of redemption is not to say that success in the argumentative practice can substitute for God's grace or is equivalent to an existential acceptance of it. The former no more implies the latter than critical debate about the general principles of our moral obligation implies that success in moral theory can substitute for the ground of those principles or make one a virtuous person.

To the contrary, having Christian faith is one thing, and validating the beliefs by which Christian faith is characterized is something else, just as, for the Stoics, the love of wisdom is one thing and philosophical discourse is another. In keeping with this difference, let me emphasize that the "way of reason," as I use that term in this work, does *not* designate a way of life in the sense that Christian faith and, on Hadot's interpretation, ancient philosophy represent ways of life. Rather, the "way of reason" designates solely an argumentative practice in or through which beliefs that have been contested or called into question may be validated or invalidated.

But if the difference between Christian faith and the ancient love of wisdom conditioned early Christian accounts of reason, the difference between faith as a response to God's love and philosophy as a kind of critical discourse was certainly clear to many major theologians in the Christian tradition. Hadot himself remarks that "philosophy in the Middle Ages had become a purely theoretical and abstract activity. . . . no longer a way of life," in part because of the emergence of medieval universities. Philosophy was now understood as the servant of theology, and supplied "the conceptual, logical, physical, and metaphysical materials it needed" (Hadot: 270). In this regard, as in so many others, Thomas Aquinas is exemplary. Yet Aquinas also exemplifies the dominating insistence of Christian theology on limits to reason, now understood as the way of validating or invalidating claims to truth by argument. So, we are led to ask: Given this conception of philosophy as solely theoretical reasoning, why have Christian thinkers nonetheless denied to it the possibility of validating Christian belief? Differences between Christian faith and philosophy as a way of life may have been important to early thinkers and may have had a continuing effect. But we do not begin to measure the minds of Aquinas and other subsequent theologians (or of early Christian thinkers themselves) if we suppose that this circumstance could be controlling in the absence of other conditions. Whatever else is involved, I suggest, those other conditions include the profound influence exercised by Greek philosophy in the theoretical sense, that is, by the conceptual materials inherited from classical Greek metaphysics.

This may seem to be an unlikely suggestion. As already noted, Greek commitment to philosophy as a way of life included the affirmation, some would say the discovery, that the world and human life is, by nature, rational. Thus, the legacy of Greek conceptual achievements might seem more or less directly opposed to the majority voice of Christian theology. As appropriated in Christian thought, however, a definitive feature of this inheritance in fact dictated that Christian theism could not be redeemed by the way of reason. I have in mind the metaphysical idea that change or the capacity to change is a mark of imperfection, and thus a supreme being or kind of being must be entirely changeless. Moreover, change and temporality require each other. "Without motion and change," Augustine rightly said, "there is no time, while in eternity there is no change" (1984: 435). Hence, a perfect reality or kind of reality must be completely eternal, and only lesser things can be temporal. As a context for Christian explication, this fundamental conception means that God as the ultimate source and end of all things must be wholly changeless or eternal, and time itself must be a condition created by God with the creation of all else. "God, in whose eternity there is no change at all," Augustine concluded, "is the creator and director of time" (1984: 435).

Having so formulated the difference between God and all other things, Christian thinkers were, so far as I can see, bound also to conclude that Christian theism cannot be fully validated by argument. This follows because God's nature, understood as the completely eternal source and end of all else, cannot be argumentatively established.

The conclusion becomes more apparent, perhaps, when we note that "eternal" does not mean "everlasting" or "present throughout all time" but, rather, "nontemporal." To be sure, medieval theologians also used other terms to designate God's perfection; for instance, God was said to be without complexity and thus the completely "simple" totality of all things. Just as eternity could only be thought of as not temporal, however, so God's simplicity could only be designated as not complex. More generally, philosophy could designate God's nature literally only by negations, as the theological tradition has largely asserted. So far as literal speaking goes, God's perfection could only be incomprehensible.

But a divine reality whose nature is in this way mysterious, that is, a reality to which no positive terms literally apply, cannot be explicated and defended by reason alone. I am mindful that a minority of Christian thinkers, including some prior to the modern age, have sought to provide that explication and defense. Those attempts are contributions to Western philosophical theology that have persisted throughout the Common Era and into the present day.[4] Hence, I can only summarily assert here that, to the best of my reasoning, understandings of a highest being or highest kind of being said to be completely changeless cannot be redeemed by argument – again because "changeless" also designates only by negation. If this summary judgment is correct, the dominant tradition of Christian thought rightly inferred that knowledge of God, conceived as completely eternal, is not fully accessible to reason.

---

4. Anselm's so-called ontological argument for the existence of "that than which nothing greater can be conceived" is, perhaps, the classic example, the more so because Anselm also sought to establish by argument the nature or attributes of the greatest possible being (see Anselm). Aquinas held, at least on the traditional reading of him, that natural reason can demonstrate the existence of a completely eternal "beginning of things and their last end" (S.T. 1.2. introduction) but, against Anselm, cannot know God's essence – or, as Aquinas also said, we can, without the special revelation of God, know that God exists but not what God is (see S.C.G. 3.39.1). In asserting that natural knowledge "cannot... see the essence of God" (S.T. 1.12.12), Aquinas insofar gave one classical expression to the majority voice. My own view is that arguments for God's existence cannot be successful if, with both Anselm and Aquinas, the beginning and last end of all things is completely eternal. This conception entails, as mentioned in the text and as Aquinas made clear, that God can be literally designated only by negation, and even terms like "the beginning of things and their last end" have no positive literal meaning. But without speaking literally of what God is, no theistic argument can successfully conclude that the existence of something, in distinction from sheer nothing, has been demonstrated. I have discussed Aquinas's position at greater length in Gamwell 2001.

Still, this explanation of the majority voice, some might correctly note, is deficient in the following way: Inferring that Christian theism cannot be fully redeemed by argument does not entail that adequate knowledge of reality and human life as such transcends reason. One could conclude instead that Christian faith is not true. Naturally, a Christian thinker who draws this conclusion might be led to cease living as a Christian. Accordingly, the conclusion may be especially difficult to reach. One's religious belief answers the question about ultimate worth, thereby serving in principle to integrate all of one's beliefs, and thus may be especially resistant to change. Still, this cannot mean that no Christian can decide through reflection against the credibility of her or his religious belief, at least if, as our attempted explanation here presupposes, that conviction can indeed be argumentatively assessed. Hence, the fact that earlier thinkers continued to confess their Christian faith, in spite of placing it beyond rational validation, shows that they chose one of two possible options. They rejected the way of reason in order not to reject Christian faith. But why this choice? Some further accounting is needed.

Their choice, I believe, can also be understood in terms of the resources inherited from Greek metaphysics. That legacy not only conditioned Christian theological statements but also pervaded, at least until the modern period, the context in which alternative views of reality and human life were or might be formulated. Let us accept that the fundamental comparison in this metaphysics, namely, what can change is a lesser reality and what cannot is the eminent reality, is itself finally indefensible. The hegemony of this inheritance then means that all available alternatives were more or less equally problematic. But one could not in this situation simply suspend belief. The question to which Christian faith and its alternatives are answers is the fundamental question about how to live, and humans cannot suspend leading their lives. Accordingly, thinkers already committed to the way of Christian faith took themselves to be, and perhaps were, justified in believing that true religious belief cannot be fully redeemed by argument. Indeed, we might be more persuaded to credit their course if we hold that the Christian claim can, against their conclusion, be redeemed by argument. This implies that earlier Christian thinkers were, with whatever limitations their conceptual resources imposed, seeking to explicate an apprehension of the abiding truth about human life.

Obviously, this brief discussion of how Greek conceptual resources influenced Christian thought has not included the examination of particular Christian thinkers through which the explanation offered might be confirmed or falsified. I have only proposed that the logic of those resources helps to explain the majority voice and, in that sense, have only proposed a hypothesis to be tested. I will not pursue an engagement with medieval theology, much less pursue the full treatment of cultural and institutional circumstances required adequately to explain why the majority voice has dominated Christian thought. My comments here can only suggest the kind of historical interpretation through which Christians today might credit that voice even while they depart from it by affirming in our context the way of reason. But if the proposed account is right as far as it goes, we can draw another conclusion: The humanistic commitment could become pervasive in the modern age only because it increasingly pursued alternatives to the whole Greek metaphysical legacy. As discussed in the previous chapter, modernity's commitment to reason was largely inseparable from the discrediting of medieval metaphysics. Indeed, democracy emerged only because modern thought denied the predetermined hierarchy of beings and the corresponding stratification of society that medieval thought grounded in the eternal law of God conceived as completely changeless. If that concept of God is finally indefensible, it also follows that Christian faith cannot be redeemed by the way of reason unless its theistic belief does not require a completely eternal reality. An alternative understanding of God is, I believe, not only possible but also more appropriate to Christian belief. But I will defer discussion of this alternative until the next chapter, which will ask about the substantive principles of justice and the common good included in or implied by the meaning of Christian faith.

III DISCOURSE AS A CHRISTIAN COMMITMENT

Even if departure from most previous Christian witness does not prevent Christian commitment to the way of reason, we have not yet shown that Christian faith allows that commitment and, insofar, democratic political rule. For all that has been said, the majority voice may in fact express the abiding meaning of the Christian confession.

Many contemporary Christians continue to share that understanding of their faith. Further, many modern Christian thinkers have argued in differing ways that this understanding is consistent with the democratic way.[5] But if democracy means popular sovereignty, to repeat again the conclusion of Chapter 2, these attempts cannot succeed. On its only coherent meaning, government by the people is rule through full and free discourse.

In order to confirm the point, let us suppose for the moment that Christian belief cannot be validated or invalidated by the way of reason and, therefore, the ultimate terms of political assessment cannot be redeemed by argument. It then follows, so far as I can see, that Christian belief provides no principled basis for popular participation in governmental decision making unless the political community includes an established religion. If valid political assessments finally depend on terms whose determination transcends full and free discourse, decisions involving all the people cannot be good or right, except accidentally, unless the people, or at least most of them, reach their individual assessments through some other access to those ultimate terms. Hence, the true understanding of ultimate worth must be stipulated in the constitution and inculcated or taught by the state.

Citizens in that community might still disagree about which particular laws and policies exemplify the fundamental principles affirmed by the Christian faith. Thus, there may still be much to debate. But this does not gainsay that the state stipulates to all citizens the ultimate terms of political assessment, so that, whatever popular participation there may be, popular sovereignty is violated. To be sure, Christians in a given modern society might find that circumstances currently prevent constitutional endorsement of their conviction – because, say, they are a political minority. Nonetheless, their confession, without the humanistic commitment, implies an established religion. Their goal in the longer run should be to make that establishment a reality, as some Christians today who accept the majority voice seem to concede. In principle, then, a commitment to government in which final

---

5. Perhaps the most influential attempts to make this case, at least in the United States, are those of Reinhold Niebuhr and John Courtney Murray (see Niebuhr 1944; Murray).

authority belongs to the people is inconsistent with the meaning of Christian faith.[6]

Whether contemporary Christians must accept this outcome cannot be conclusively determined without a more or less complete interpretation of the confession that Jesus is the Christ. In our discussion heretofore, I have taken its essential meaning to include the following: Jesus decisively reveals God, the ultimate source of all things and the ultimate ground of worth, as all-embracing love, who calls all women and men to love this God without reservation and, thereby, to have their every purpose express love for all the world God loves. For Christians, this calling is the Great Commandment because it is, finally, the only commandment, in the sense that all others are applications or articulations of it. In order to answer our present question, I will continue the assumption that anything else within the abiding content of Christian faith must be everywhere or in all circumstances consistent with this affirmation of God and the divine purpose. Given this premise, I will argue that the essence of Christian faith not only allows but also prescribes the humanistic commitment.

We can start toward this conclusion through the belief that God's call or commandment is addressed to all women and men. It defines for every human individual the good to which her or his every purpose should be directed – or defines, as we may say, her or his authenticity. Since every person is commanded to live authentically, God's call also presents a choice, that is, a decision of faith she or

---

6. I recognize that some Christians in American history, sharing the majority voice, have hoped for or expected what has been called a de facto establishment, in distinction from official state support for their religion. On this view, perhaps associated above all with evangelical revivals in the early nineteenth century, voluntary conversion to Christianity becomes sufficiently widespread in the society that political assessments of the majority in fact take their bearings from ultimate terms that are Christian. A democratic constitution and its principle of religious freedom is then seen as proper because acceptance of the Christian faith must be voluntary, and the political community will be what it should be only through pervasive but non-coerced Christian commitment. But this supposed harmony of democracy and the majority voice suffers because the prescription of religious freedom itself derives from the proposed account of Christian faith. That there should be no de jure establishment because Christian belief, which cannot be validated by argument, must be voluntarily accepted is itself a reading of the constitution that depends on the suprarational truth of Christianity. Hence, there are no public grounds for adherents of all religions to endorse a democratic constitution. Citizens generally could not have a principled basis for accepting religious freedom unless they are taught its specifically Christian meaning, so that this view, against itself, implies a de jure established religion.

he ought to make. Each is called to love God without reservation instead of living as if something else confers ultimate worth and defines the inclusive purpose of life. But this means that every human in every moment must be aware of God's all-embracing love and purpose. That elemental fact of human life follows from Christian belief because "ought implies can." This dictum, familiar in moral theory, states that no individual can be obligated to decide for a given action or purpose unless that choice is one of her or his real alternatives. Moreover, a real alternative cannot be prescribed unless the individual is both aware of it and, still further, believes it to be prescribed. A person cannot decide in accord with a prescription unless she or he is aware of the obligation. If one does not believe the choice to be prescribed, one cannot choose it because one ought to do so.

Having this belief does not erase the possibility that one fails to make that choice. But a decision cannot be immoral unless the person who makes it is somehow aware that it is wrong. Moral thought throughout Western history has largely agreed that immorality is in this way self-convicting because a person is not morally responsible for decisions taken in ignorance, except when or insofar as failure to understand is itself something for which she or he is culpable. Our criminal jurisprudence joins this consensus by excusing a defendant for her or his alleged misdeed if she or he did not know right from wrong. Hence, the Christian conviction that all humans ought always to decide in accord with the divine purpose implies that all humans are aware of God's purpose as defining their authenticity. Whatever else Christian faith means, it asserts that God is omnipresent in human experience or present in common human experience.

It may seem both implausible and impertinent to say that all humans are aware of God's all-embracing love and see in God's purpose their authenticity. There is a perfectly straightforward sense in which many people do not believe in this God or, for that matter, any God. Nonetheless, God's love is, for Christians, the ultimate source and end of all things, and their conviction would be false if any human could experience anything at all without also experiencing this ultimate ground. Moreover, the Christian account of human life need not mean that God's inescapable presence is always present to explicit attention. Indeed, a given individual might be always aware and yet never explicitly conscious of the divine reality. "Present to explicit attention" here means the content within the clear center of one's consciousness – in the way that, for instance, a story one is reading is then the focus of attention or a task in which one is engaged is then typically clear in one's mind. Most humans most of the time have no such focused awareness of God and many people never do, and this is the straightforward sense in which there is no universal belief in God.

But our conscious lives are not exhausted by our explicit attention. Clear consciousness is, in the nature of the case, the most apparent form of understanding. Still, we can easily recognize the dim background or deeper level of understandings not in focus, which always surrounds and contributes the indispensable setting for our interest in whatever dominates our attention. Just as Mona Lisa's smile would not be intriguing except against the background of her visage and bearing, so explicit attention always depends on the vague awareness of things present but not perspicuous. For instance, comprehending the Gettysburg Address would be impossible without background understandings of American history, politics, war, English rhetoric, and the language itself that we previously learned and now take for granted because at the moment they are not at the center of consciousness – and the more extensive these background understandings, the more profound our appreciation of Lincoln's genius.

The fundamental decisions of all humans to which Christian belief refers occur at this deeper level of consciousness, and one confirmation of this reading is our common recognition that we never know clearly the full reasons or motivations for what we do. Whatever is or is not explicitly in view, and whatever other background understandings one has or has not acquired, Christian belief implies that we could not live with understanding at all unless at the deepest level we were aware of the ultimate source and end of everything else we might possibly understand. Saying that God is present in common human experience means only that consciousness of God's purpose and decision for or against one's authenticity cannot be absent from the surrounding background of awareness. The experience of God is "an overtone implied in all experience" (Niebuhr 1941–3: I, 127) or, as I will say, all human existence includes a primal belief in God.

Human life, we can also say, occurs by way of a primal decision for some self-understanding. To choose consciously some purpose or action is to determine with understanding what one is or becomes and thus to decide for a self-understanding. Yet, our conscious lives proceed much of the time without focused attention to how we understand ourselves or to the decisions we are making. Instead, the understanding of self is chosen in the deeper context of awareness. When our decisions come into focus, moreover, we typically attend to specific alternatives that our present situation leaves open to us. In any case, to be human is to choose consciously among specific alternatives for purpose, and, on the Christian account, this choice involves or includes a deep decision addressed to the primal issue of our existence: whether or not to understand ourselves as persons whose worth depends entirely on the God of all-embracing love and, therefore, whose authenticity is found in service to God's purpose. Precisely because this primal decision is among real alternatives, we humans everywhere and always understand God and believe that the divine purpose defines the choice we ought to make. This abiding human condition not only follows from God's universal calling but also is implied by the God who calls, in the sense that all-embracing love could not deny any human the opportunity to live authentically by loving God with all her or his heart and soul and mind and strength.

Some may question this explication of the Christian confession because it seems to deny any importance to the Christian religion. If belief in God is inseparable from our primal decision for a self-understanding, then the revelation of God through Jesus Christ seems to be merely repetitious of God's primal self-disclosure to all humans. So far as I can see, Christian faith does indeed mean that Jesus Christ decisively re-presents or presents again the ultimate reality, since the God said to be revealed through him can only be a God present everywhere. But Christians do not thereby deny the importance of Christian faith, because the disclosure through Jesus Christ is an *explicit* re-presentation of the primal presence without which there could be no distinctively human life at all. Since decision for or against our authenticity occurs beyond the reach of explicit attention, we humans are aided by a re-presentation of the truth. Through explicit or focused attention on Jesus as the Christ, Christians intend to help cultivate authenticity in their deepest selves. Their religious activities, we can say, are those specific practices through which Christians seek to persuade their own primal decisions, so that they then choose in all they do to understand themselves in service to the divine purpose. Thus, the special importance of the Christian religion, its symbols and practices, consists in its making explicit again and again the revelation of God through Jesus Christ.

In their witness of faith, Christians claim truth for this re-presentation of God. They assert that the ultimate ground of worth present everywhere is none other than the God explicitly revealed through Jesus Christ. What we currently seek to know, then, is whether that faith affirms, the majority voice notwithstanding, argumentative assessment of this claim.[7] A positive answer to that question is now readily available. If something substantially like the preceding account of human existence and the Christian religion follows from Christian faith itself, the abiding content of that faith gives no reason to refuse the humanistic commitment. Because their faith means that God as re-presented through Jesus Christ is present to and understood by all humans, Christians may without pause pledge that this faith can be redeemed through reasons authorized by common human experience.

Given its importance to the present work, this conclusion should be underscored. For Christians, Jesus Christ re-presents explicitly the

7. Perhaps this will suggest that, in another way, the humanistic commitment denies the importance of Christianity. If the truth of Christian faith can be established by argument, then humans can, by the way of reason, know God and the character of human life *explicitly;* hence, the Christian religion, even with respect to our explicit awareness, serves no purpose. But this new objection confuses the function of Christian religion with that of critical reflection or discourse. As mentioned, the religious activities of Christians serve to cultivate belief at the deepest level of consciousness or to persuade their deepest selves to make authentic decisions. Hence, activities of the church include attention to highly symbolic expressions and practices having the power to evoke loyalty to the divine purpose. The function of these activities, we can say, assumes the truth of Christian faith. Discourse has another function. If Christians affirm it, argument becomes important to them when, for whatever reasons, they come to question whether the faith expressed in Christian symbols and practices is indeed true. Hence, reflection in this sense cannot assume the truth of Christian faith and cannot substitute for religious activities. Instead, the way of reason serves Christians as they decide whether to continue believing that Jesus is the Christ or seek to continue living without troubling doubts about the validity of their confession.

We should add that critical reflection also becomes important when, for whatever reasons, Christians come to question whether their understanding of Christian faith is appropriate to Jesus Christ. For this kind of reflection, however, the criterion is not common human experience and reason but, rather, the primary norm for expressions of what Christian confession means. Moreover, the question of appropriate understanding is theologically prior to asking about the validity of Christian faith, because one cannot rightly assess the Christian confession without knowing what it takes to be true. Our present discussion in the text, asking whether Christian faith affirms the humanistic commitment, intends to exemplify this prior kind of critical reflection. For the distinctions here among primal self-understanding, religion, and critical reflection, I am indebted to the systematic theology of Schubert M. Ogden (see Ogden 1982, 1992).

love and calling of God that humans experience everywhere. In this sense, Christian faith presents again the primal belief about reality and human authenticity all humans always share, the "overtone implied in all experience" (Niebuhr 1941–3: I, 127). This means that any other belief or understanding, wherever it occurs and whatever its particular content, implies the Christian understanding of this primal belief. But argument or reasoning, whatever else it involves, proceeds by making explicit the implications of statements or understandings. Hence, Christian faith, if it is true, can be validated by argument, namely, by pursuing the implications common to all possible beliefs or understandings and thereby reaching common human experience. Critical assessment of Christian belief is possible through reasons authorized when they explicate what must be the case wherever life with understanding occurs. In this respect, "the appeal to reason" is for Christian faith itself "that ultimate judge, universal and yet individual to each, to which all authority must bow" (Whitehead 1961: 162). It now follows that Christian faith not only permits but also prescribes the humanistic commitment. To refuse it is to deny that God is revealed to all humans in their primal decision for a self-understanding. The majority voice, however justified in certain cultural conditions, cannot belong to the abiding content of Christian faith.

For all that, however, even some modern theological proposals come to a different conclusion, and it may be useful to review why. The reflections here on faith and reason, they object, falsely assume that reason can reach the content of our primal belief. Within the past two centuries, many Christian thinkers have affirmed God's presence in common human experience and, further, reason's capacity to confirm our inescapable awareness of some transcendent reality. More often than not, however, they have also echoed the majority voice by denying that reason has the power to discover God's nature. Friedrich Schleiermacher, for instance, held that all humans share a "consciousness of absolute dependence" but denied that reason can determine the ultimate "*Whence*" on which we depend (Schleiermacher: 16). A substantial theological tradition influenced by Schleiermacher has advanced a similar reading. For Paul Tillich, to choose one example, "pure reason" can show that all humans have an "ultimate concern," but the proper object of this concern cannot be determined philosophically (Tillich: 23, 24).

Those who defend this position do not deny that we can and do explicitly entertain and formulate understandings of God's nature. To the contrary, specifically religious activities do or may involve precisely such explicit attention because they function to re-present our primal relation to God and, thereby, to influence our deepest decisions. But claims to validity for these explicit expressions cannot be validated by discourse, we are told, because the nature of God cannot be reached by seeking the implications common to all human understanding or experience. Typically, these thinkers insist that designations of God's nature cannot achieve the kind of literal formulation required by argumentative assessment. We can only designate or speak of God rightly by way of symbols or myths or analogical terms associated with the Christian religion and, perhaps, those of some other religious communities or traditions.

Adequate discussion of this view would require engagement with some major figures in recent and more distant philosophical theology and thus would also take us through an extensive detour. I will simply state the summary reason why, so far as I can see, any such reading of our condition must be mistaken: Agreeing that all human life implies a relation to God but denying that God's nature can be known by the way of reason, these thinkers argue for a primal belief to which argument can give no content. But a belief that has no content cannot be distinguished from the absence of belief. To be sure, the proposal affirms that our primal relation to God does indeed have content, denying only that argument can uncover it. But this means that reason can demonstrate the presence of a belief even while remaining blind to what is believed. We are then bound to ask: So far as reason is concerned, what is the difference between this belief and a supposed belief that really does not exist because it has no content at all? No convincing answer can be given because, in each case, the belief is empty.

Unless it can show *what* the ultimate ground of worth is, in other words, argument could never show that we have an awareness of it. But Christian faith means that argument *can* show the latter, because the God whose love calls all humans must be present in common human experience – and this much the modern theologians in question concede. Notwithstanding how often their position has been asserted, I conclude that affirmation of God's omnipresence prescribes the humanistic commitment. For whatever it is worth, I will also express the following judgment: Many theologians, beginning with Schleiermacher, have compromised this commitment, even while they affirm universal consciousness of God, because they continue to conceive of God as the completely eternal reality, of which we can speak literally only by negation. That is why speaking positively of God must be by way of symbols or myths or analogies. But if their conception requires denial of the way of reason, this only means that their conception cannot be valid. Because Christian faith implies a primal belief in God, the truth of Christian faith depends on an understanding of God's nature that argument can validate. At least in this respect, Christians have no cause to resist and every reason to embrace full and free discourse as a form of political rule.

Chapter 4

Justice in the Community of Love

A brief summary of the previous two chapters will be useful in setting the stage for this one. Seeking clarity about politics as a Christian vocation, we asked about the nature of democracy as a form of political community. Having answered that government by the people makes sense only as a full and free political discourse, we were led to ask whether Christian faith includes the humanistic commitment. I have commended a positive answer. The God in whom Christians believe is necessarily present to all humans, calling them to love God without reservation. Hence, Christian belief can be assessed through reasons authorized by common human experience, and Christian faith prescribes the humanistic commitment. Once this commitment is accepted, moreover, there is no principled way to stop the drive to popular sovereignty. Any attempt to arrest it is bound to assert grounds for political inequality, and reason does not privilege persons but solely claims that can be redeemed by argument. The modern affirmation of reason and the emergence of democracy are not only historically connected but also wedded by logic. If it prescribes the humanistic commitment, Christian faith insofar mandates government by the people.

To be sure, democracy cannot be prescribed unless it is a real possibility, and some argue that popular sovereignty waits on certain economic and social prerequisites. For instance, a community most of whose members suffer severe poverty and illiteracy cannot in fact be ruled by the many. Some other form of political decision making is required, even if those decisions should pursue conditions in which democracy becomes possible. I will not pause to assess this line of thought and, instead, will simply assume that any merit it may have is not relevant to our situation. The present work, in other words, asks about the political meaning of Christian faith in circumstances where economic and social preconditions for popular sovereignty do in fact obtain.

Nonetheless, all we have said remains insufficient to show that Christian faith prescribes democracy – or, at least, does so consistently. Although Christians should endorse the humanistic commitment, of which popular sovereignty is the implied political form, we can still ask whether Christian belief in God is *substantively* consistent with the democratic political process. Toward seeing what is at stake here, we may review briefly our previous account of a democratic constitution. The constitutional provisions of government by the people are, I said, properly exhausted by formative principles of justice. Adherence to these principles is explicitly neutral to any possible political disagreement because they define the ethics of citizenship as the practice of political discourse about all contested claims. We also noted that democracy cannot be a sensible form of political community unless some substantive principle or principles of justice are valid. An argumentative practice cannot occur without something about which participants may sensibly argue, and a full and free political discourse is pointless unless principles by which laws and policies of the state are properly determined can be redeemed through discussion and debate among "we the people."

The last point has the following important consequence: The moral validity of formative principles themselves finally depends on the valid substantive principle or principles. This means simply that democracy as a form of political rule can itself be morally assessed only by appeal to ultimate terms of political assessment. Thus, we cannot finally defend a democratic constitution as morally valid without a valid substantive principle or principles by which the constitutional principles are authorized. Saying this does not compromise the difference between formative and substantive principles. The constitution should not stipulate what the ultimate terms of political assessment are; rather, explicit consideration of them belongs entirely to the constituted discussion and debate. What the constitution explicitly says is one thing, and what its validity presupposes is something else – just as it is one thing for friends with basic moral disagreements to treat each other with respect and something else for them to determine what basic principle provides the full sanction for their civility.

A democratic constitution, we can say, makes no sense without a substantive moral backing, even while it remains explicitly neutral to what that backing is. To capture this point, let us say that democratic justice has a twofold or compound character – including, on the one hand, formative or constitutional principles and, on the other, the substantive principle or set of principles that provides terms for all political assessment. Since the formative principles are themselves backed by those terms, this distinction must itself be prescribed by the substantive principle or principles. In its fullest sense, justice can be democratic in character only if it includes as a part of itself the prescription of full and free political discourse. Thereby, the former provides the moral grounds for a constitution, adherence to which is explicitly neutral even to disagreement about the substantive principle or principles in question. If analogies are helpful, we can revise the one suggested a moment ago. True friendship includes the civility with which friends treat each other and is, it might be said, the full human relationship civility is meant to promote, even while civility can also be exhibited in relations otherwise characterized by mutual antagonism. In a roughly similar way, the complete character of justice is compound, prescribing a full and free political discourse as an aspect of itself.

We can now see more clearly why the previous chapters do not themselves show that Christian faith prescribes democracy – or, at least, does so consistently. The substantive terms of political assessment given by a religious conviction may or may not ground the formative constitution of popular sovereignty as an aspect of themselves. Even if the humanistic commitment is accepted, the issue remains: Does the given understanding of reality and human life consistently prescribe a democratic political process? Perhaps the religious conviction in question is at odds with itself, accepting the humanistic commitment while failing to provide substantive principles that back politics by way of full and free discourse. Granting that Christian faith prescribes the way of reason, we cannot infer forthwith that Christians have a democratic political vocation without having in place their understanding of God and the divine purpose and the political principles it implies. The present chapter seeks this understanding. Christian faith includes, I will argue, a substantive principle of justice by which popular sovereignty is grounded. In the process of reaching that conclusion, we will also define the ultimate terms of assessment with which contemporary Christians can deliberate about their political purposes.

I THE COMMUNITY OF LOVE

To state the matter in its most general sense, we need now to clarify the Christian idea of or, better, ideal for community. In question here is not the specifically Christian community but, rather, the larger human community of which the church is a part. Politics governs this larger community, and the proper character of political purpose depends on what human community in all of its aspects should be or become. Principles of justice, we can say, articulate human community at its best in terms of the order rightly provided or promoted through government; principles of justice assign to politics its part in the good community. To be sure, "justice" is sometimes used in a broader sense, whereby it designates the proper character of any and all human association or the good community in all its forms. Aquinas spoke in this way when he said, following the classical definition, that justice is "the act of rendering his due to each man" (S.T. 2–2.58.4). Since our focus is politics, however, I will reserve the term "justice" for the order with which activities of the state are concerned and, therefore, will distinguish between the character of a good community and its principles of justice. Still, a Christian account of justice in this more narrow sense articulates for activities of the state the Christian ideal for human community. Hence, we must first identify the latter.

I begin by recalling once more the meaning of Christian faith from which previous discussions have taken their bearings: Jesus decisively reveals the ultimate source and end of all things as the God of all-embracing love, who calls us to unreserved love for God and, thereby, for all the world God loves. This calling, we have said, is addressed *to* all humans; it defines the authentic human life as such and thus the abiding purpose that ought to be chosen in every moment of human decision. We are called to love our neighbors, that is, all others, as ourselves, so that each individual becomes someone who both loves and is loved by others. Universalizing the call in this way may be taken as a summary statement of the Christian ideal for community. Humans are to live together as a community of love.

Saying this alone, however, will not secure a basis for political principles. We need to unpack the nature of this community. Toward that end, the decisive point is this: Our call to common love is an expression of God's love for us. The command is not imposed in order to exploit or debase humans but is, rather, given by a God who wills us good, who wills for all the good life. Here, "the good life" does not mean simply a moral life, in the sense that a person lives in conformity with God's commandment, however essential that may be. Rather, God wills for each a life that is full or flourishing or is, in the classical sense, happy. "The good life" means the kind of life loving parents wish for their children (see Urmson: 12). Hence, Christian faith implies that a flourishing or happy life occurs in or through participation in a community of love. "The individual," wrote Reinhold Niebuhr, "is related to the community . . . in such a way that the highest reaches of his individuality are dependent on the social substance out of which they arise and they must find their end and fulfillment in the community" (Niebuhr 1944: 48). Within this world, the principal source and inclusive end of the good life is human mutuality.

We can clarify this point be relating both mutuality and the good life to the primal decision for a self-understanding, for which God's call presents the authentic alternative. This course requires, however, some further attention to what and how we decide. As discussed earlier, to have a self-understanding is to answer the question of inclusive purpose. Either a person accepts God's call or instead understands herself or himself as if something else sets the purpose all other purposes ought to serve. To believe that nation or race or family, or one's own power or prestige or pleasure, or anything other than God defines one's ultimate end is to be fundamentally at fault. Whether authentic or not, one's self-understanding is primal in the sense that every human in every moment leads her or his life by way of decision for it. However deep in the background of consciousness, it determines what the given person becomes at a given moment or through a given activity.

Consider now that each moment or activity becomes something particular, because this fact reveals another important feature of our lives. Always occurring at some time and place or within some given setting, the decision for an inclusive purpose is always simultaneously the choice of some specific purpose. Clearly, the latter cannot be anything one pleases; rather, it must be within the range of possibilities offered but also restricted by a person's particular setting. A person in California has options for the afternoon, but they do not include a visit to Rome. An ordinary citizen may decide for whom to campaign and vote but cannot decide, absent changed circumstances, to speak in a congressional debate. An illiterate person may seek an education but cannot choose here and now to practice law.

Living with understanding, we decide among the specific alternatives open at any given time and place by evaluating them as better or worse, even if this assessment is also in the background of consciousness. Each specific purpose, then, involves the primal decision in the following way: The terms for evaluation are given by our simultaneous decision for an inclusive purpose, to which all others should contribute. In so describing human activity, I do not suggest a deliberative process. Deliberation is, to be sure, an important part of life with understanding and is often significant as a process leading up to the moment in question. But each present activity within its particular context, which may include previous deliberation, chooses at one and the same time both an inclusive and a specific purpose. The former could not be chosen except as the basis for assessing specific alternatives, and the latter could not be chosen without a decision for ultimate terms of evaluation.

Let us continue to focus on the specific purpose and, especially, on the possibilities open for it. As already suggested, decision in the present moment cannot affect the range of those possibilities. Choice occurs within the limits set by the given context or, more precisely, by the particular past a person then inherits – although each decision will alter the context for the next moment. A person's life, we can say, is her or his developing course or career of self-conscious activities, each of which begins with relation to the given past. What a person becomes at any given moment is, then, the consequence in part of conditions she or he inherits. Notable within this legacy are her or his own earlier activities. Indeed, we humans enjoy an impressive capacity to carry our own previous lives into each present, and this is why we can execute over greater or lesser periods of time immensely detailed plans or projects. But the context also includes our physical and biological setting and our associations with other people, both personal or intimate relationships and participation in larger institutional structures, insofar as all of these affect present experience. Beginning with the possibilities received through this complex inheritance, each present activity completes itself or unifies its experience by deciding for a purpose. Thereby, a new moment of human life makes a difference to the future, including the later life of the individual in question and the lives of others, by adding in its own particular way to the context for subsequent experiences.

Thinking about human life in this way, we can see that specific opportunities may vary dramatically at differing times and from person to person, depending on the context. Typically, small children face far more limited horizons than do adults. Education usually expands our opportunities, as does a past life that was disciplined or virtuous, while significant pain and distress constrict them. Other things being equal, the possibilities open to a given individual at a given time and place are enhanced insofar as she or he experiences physical and psychological well-being, economic security, settings for useful or engaging work, personal or intimate relationships of love and friendship, a rich cultural background, and supportive institutions in the larger social and political order. Alfred North Whitehead wrote that higher animal life is characterized by a "three-fold urge," not only to live but also to live well and then to live better, and that this urge "is the most prominent fact" of human existence (Whitehead 1958: 8). The chance to live better means increased possibilities for our specific purposes.

Another name for what context determines is the chance for creativity, the opportunity for more distinctive achievement. "Creativity" here does not mean simply artistic or intellectual creativity, although these illustrate the more general idea. All human activity is creative in the sense that each person in each present moment adds something to the world by choosing how her or his experience of the past will become a new unity that makes a difference. The point is, then, that possibilities for this creative achievement are more restricted or more significant, depending on the particular past one inherits. Summarily speaking, greater possibilities occur because the setting, including one's biographical past, presents to experience a more profound diversity, relations that are both complex and coordinated. Thereby the new moment is favored with potential for more distinctive unity – for higher "reaches of . . . individuality" (Niebuhr 1944: 48) – and thus for a more worthwhile effect on the world to come.

This reading implies an important distinction between two kinds of creative freedom or, perhaps better, two aspects of our creativity. On the one hand, we humans are more or less free in the measure of opportunity we receive from our given setting. On the other hand, we humans are equally free to live authentically or inauthentically, that is, by way of a self-understanding. I will speak of the first as greater or lesser emancipation, because the range of possibilities is endowed by the past, or, with the same meaning, as greater or lesser empowerment, since wider possibilities give power for greater achievement. This, then, is distinct from our primal or moral freedom, with which we decide for an inclusive purpose and thereby choose among whatever opportunities we receive. We can now say that a human individual enjoys the good life insofar as her or his continuing career of activities is more creative, so that human flourishing also has two aspects: on the one hand, a context or set of conditions that is more fully emancipating or empowers more distinctive achievement; on the other, decisions that make the most of these opportunities because they pursue the best possible future or choose an authentic self-understanding.

With this characterization at hand, let us revisit the community of love or human mutuality as the principal worldly source and inclusive worldly end of the good life God wills for all. Calling this community a source of our flourishing means that empowerment is a gift from our life together. The general nature of loving others is giving of oneself in a manner that seeks their own good; in mutual love, therefore, each receives creative opportunities from her or his relations to the others. Still, it may not be obvious that living together is the *principal* worldly context for greater emancipation, because human possibilities are compromised in the absence of favorable relations to the larger environment. Typically, at least, creative opportunity is impoverished by the want of certain biological and material conditions – for instance, a healthy body; the material conditions to protect and sustain it; and the physical, economic, and technological resources for certain higher kinds of human achievement. Moreover, one distinctive kind of human activity consists in understanding or appreciating for their own sake the natural world and its living beings.

All of this follows from saying that God loves *all* the world, which implies that human flourishing requires a kind of mutuality between the human community and the orders and creatures of its natural habitat. Within God's world, nonetheless, the good life has its principal source in human mutuality. This is so, in part, because more favorable relations to our wider environment themselves largely depend on realizing communal possibilities for providing health and safety, economic and technological resources, and opportunities to appreciate the natural world. In addition and more important, the indispensable context endowed by the wider environment is finally background for the higher reaches of creative opportunity, which are given to us through relations to other people that convey their individualities or creative achievements. Even our understanding and appreciation of nature would be trivial except as they are shaped through communication with others who have pursued these interests. Human associations of intimacy, friendship, and common purpose, including our inheritance from individuals and communities that have passed into human history, carry the possibilities for the good life in the most emphatic measure.

For this reason, we can say summarily that human mutuality is to be maximized and is, in this sense, our inclusive worldly end. We pursue this end by directing whatever opportunities we have toward a life together in which each relates to or receives in the greatest possible measure creativity achieved by others. Such mutuality is the community of love, in which all are both beneficiaries and benefactors, each empowered for the greatest possible achievement and, making the most of this opportunity, contributing to the further creativity of all. As an inclusive end, this community ratifies our dependence on the wider environment, because the same community will provide for all, insofar as it can, relations to the nonhuman world, including economic and technological resources, favoring the greatest possible mutuality among creative individuals. Since the divine purpose has no spatial or temporal boundary, moreover, the common love we are privileged to pursue cannot be confined to any special or local company of individuals or bordered by some specific temporal stretch. In principle, we are called to maximize love among all humans and in the longest possible run. We are called to emancipate all through and for the sake of maximal human mutuality.

This formulation may seem to deny that God's all-embracing love confers on our natural habitat and its living things their own intrinsic worth, not simply their importance to the human adventure. Commanded to love all that God loves, we are required to respect and esteem the nonhuman world accordingly, and failure to obey this moral imperative has become the more consequential in our contemporary world, where the capacity of human habitation to violate the ecosystems on which it depends has become acutely evident. If taken in full and proper measure, however, emancipating all through and for the sake of maximal human mutuality is, I think, a purpose consistent with God's love for all the world. This purpose prescribes that we honor the integrity of our natural habitat precisely because our aim at maximal human mutuality should be defined by the long run. Moreover, due appreciation of nature's other creatures is itself an important achievement, the sharing of which among humans increases opportunities for creativity.

I recognize that these last comments only gesture toward the more extended discussion of Christian responsibility for God's larger world that alone could make them fully convincing and without which some will find the inclusive aim at maximal human mutuality suspect. Perhaps our pursuit of this end should be constrained by something like the following principle of environmental respect: The intrinsic worth of the nonhuman world should not be violated unless doing so is required to maximize human mutuality in the long run. But I will not offer more detailed consideration of this matter. In order to move toward political principles, I will, silently taking for granted this principle of environmental respect, assume the following: The God of Christian faith calls all humans to direct their every purpose toward the community of love and, therefore, to maximize the creativity of all humans.

II THE PRINCIPLE OF JUSTICE

Speaking as we have of human mutuality may easily seem utopian or romantic because it appears blind to human weakness and, specifically, the persistent evil caused by human attachment to selfish or otherwise corrupt ends. The Christian tradition has called this our capacity for sin and, beginning at least with Augustine, has recurrently warned the civil order: Political rule will only cause greater evil without recognition that sin is an irrevocable feature of the human condition. So far from mutuality from which all benefit and to which all contribute, our life together will always be profoundly invaded by overt or covert exploitation and strife. To avoid misunderstanding, then, it is well to stress that the community of love is an ideal to be pursued. However tempered political expectations should be by awareness of human fault, and however shaped political strategies should be by realistic estimates of opposing self-interests, it remains that politics cannot assess how these considerations should affect its aims without some explicit or implicit view of the good to be pursued. Political realism is not an end but, rather, a counsel for the course toward it, and the discussion here attends to the end by which public purpose should be directed. As such, the community of love enjoins its advocates to be as wise in commitment to it as the human condition and present circumstances require. This is the point in saying that human mutuality should be maximized, meaning that the aim is always to achieve it insofar as possible.

A democratic constitution, we might note, may itself include or imply both the aim at some ideal and lucidity about moral failure. The United States Constitution, for instance, displays the latter in a carefully crafted procedure for decision making, including the selection of officials. Whatever its defects,[1] this procedure seeks so to distribute and balance power as to block or impede the domination of political decisions by narrow interests – and to permit reversal of that outcome when it occurs. But if political realism is thereby institutionalized, it coexists with the idealism articulated by the principle of religious freedom and all it implies, namely, that "we the people" can govern ourselves through full and free discourse and thus, in significant measure, determine our life together in accord with valid principles of justice and the common good. Without this idealism, moreover, the realism is vacuous. The whole point of impeding political corruption is to permit as fully as possible governance by the way of reason, and unless discourse is in some significant measure effective, no decision-making procedure can ensure against takeover by tyrants.

Still, we have not yet clarified how the substantive ideal prescribed by Christian faith relates to a democratic constitution. If our inclusive end is the community of love, does it follow that politics should be democratic? The next step toward the political meaning of Christian commitment is to identify the substantive principle or principles of justice implied by pursuit of maximal human mutuality. In moving

---

1. For a discussion of these, see Dahl.

directly to these principles, let us recall that, in this discussion, justice assigns to politics its part in the good community and thus prescribes the general order of our common life to be provided and promoted by activities of the state.

The purpose of these activities, we have said, is to unify the community as a whole by governing the associations among individuals. The state's distinctive task is, therefore, to legislate, interpret, and enforce general norms of communal order in the manner and measure justice requires. Clearly, this does not entail that all other associations should be controlled in detail by political rule. Indeed, that view of governmental authority may well be called totalitarian. Hence, one enduring question to be answered again and again in political decisions concerns the limits of governmental control, and United States politics has from the outset included a persistently effective conviction that government's principal, even sole, responsibility is to protect the liberty or freedom of all from interference by the state. This question is left open by how the state's distinctive task has been formulated. Directing it to the *general* order implies that other norms of human interaction may be properly determined by individuals in or through their diverse other associations, even while leaving undetermined what general norms should be enforced throughout associational life.

The focus on general norms also sets terms in which the community of love may be articulated as a principle or principles of justice. The ideal requires emancipating all through and for the sake of maximal human mutuality; hence, political principles prescribe for our common life insofar as together we provide or promote "general conditions of creativity." With this last phrase, I have in mind circumstances and resources that are potentially important to creative achievement by any person in the political community or potentially important just because she or he is a member of that community. In contrast, we can speak of "local conditions of creativity," those important to a certain individual or group of individuals by virtue of some more particular characteristic or interest.

If someone works for a certain business firm, for instance, a share of its income and, arguably, some form of participation in its organizational decisions are local conditions of her or his creativity. On the other hand, access to work and income through some or other enterprise and, arguably, participation in the decision making of the relevant organization could be generally important. Refinement of life patterns characteristic of a given racial or ethnic group may be locally important to many of its members, while the opportunity to cultivate one's own cultural identity, whatever that is, is potentially important to any member of the political community. The conditions important to artists are different from those important to scientists or construction workers, and all three are different from those important to sports enthusiasts or lovers of music. But some conditions could be important to any occupation or project – for instance, income with which to acquire the relevant resources; access to education on the basis of which to choose a particular interest and, having chosen it, pursue it; and freedom of association that allows engagement in various pursuits with others who make similar choices.

Taking this distinction to be sufficiently clear, we can, I expect, readily agree that general conditions of creativity embrace physical and psychological well-being, including good habits; economic provision and opportunity; educational attainment and opportunity; a rich cultural context; beauty and integrity in the nonhuman world, both natural and artificial; and, implicated by all these as well as for its own sake, a favorable pattern of human association, including freedom of association. Such conditions are, then, the subject matter of justice, the sources of empowerment with which general norms of order should be concerned. Since the community of love calls for maximal emancipation of all, Christian faith implies that justice maximizes the measure of these conditions to which every individual has access.

This does not entail that all individuals should have equal access to these conditions. Some inequalities of, say, income or educational opportunity, may be prescribed or permitted because, thereby, the extent to which every individual benefits from general conditions of creativity is increased. Let us call the measure of those conditions available to those least favored the measure to which everyone has the same or equal access. For instance, if high school is open to all and higher education to some, then the former defines the measure in which education is equally available. We can now formulate as an implication of Christian faith the following substantive principle of justice: Maximize the measure of general conditions of creativity that is equally available to all – or, more concisely, *maximize the general conditions of creativity to which all have equal access.*[2] To the extent that those conditions are enjoyed by all, the common good in its politically relevant sense has been realized, and general norms for communal order should be politically defined and enforced precisely insofar as required to maximize this common good. Thereby, politics will have done what it can to maximize human mutuality.

For short, let us call this the principle of "justice as general emancipation," taking the term "general" to stand for both the kind of conditions with which justice is concerned and its aim at the maximal measure in which these conditions are generally or equally available. Naturally, much more needs to be said before this principle will serve particular judgments about a wide range of political issues. For instance, a more complete treatment should discuss the importance each person's own past decisions have for her or his present possibilities, from which it follows that the state should in appropriate ways hold individuals responsible for themselves insofar as their setting allows them to be. Relations among the many differing general conditions of creativity also require further attention. Some of these may be competitive with others, so that justice cannot mean maximizing the measure of each that is equally available. For instance, economic provision may be lessened by enhancing environmental beauty or integrity; resources for educating all members of the community may be lessened by increasing access to health care; and freedom of association may at some point be in conflict with increasing the extent to which any other general condition is equally available.

Here, however, we might be excused from pursuing these or other matters involved in fixing as fully as possible the principled terms for substantive political judgments. We have sought to identify justice within the ideal community of love in order to determine whether the Christian faith prescribes, at least in our setting, a democratic

---

2. This formulation is indebted to the political thought of John Rawls, whose singular contribution to twentieth-century political theory included his "general conception of justice," namely, that "all social primary goods – liberty and opportunity, income and wealth, and the social bases of self-respect – are to be distributed equally unless an unequal distribution of any or all of these goods is to the advantage of the least favored" (1971: 303). There are significant differences between what Rawls means by "social primary goods" and what the present discussion means by "general conditions of creativity" and, as a consequence, between the political theory he developed and the conception of justice summarily articulated here. But his commitment to maximizing the advantage of the least advantaged has been profoundly important to my own formulation.

political community, and the summary principle of justice we have reached will prove sufficient to answer this question. Returning to it, we may usefully remind ourselves of the background against which it is posed. Because Christian faith prescribes the humanistic commitment, Christian have, in this respect, no cause to resist government by the people or politics through full and free discourse. Given that conclusion, we asked whether Christian faith also implies substantive terms of political assessment by which democracy is prescribed. Hence, the issue now is whether justice as general emancipation and, behind it, the ideal community of love prescribe popular sovereignty. That the answer to this question is clearly positive will become apparent if we say something further about the rights a properly democratic constitution protects.

This constitution should stipulate the rights by which all citizens are defined as equal participants in political discourse, that is, the rights each person must have as someone whose sovereignty over her or his assessment of every political claim is equally important in political rule. To be an actual participant in political discourse, a citizen requires the familiar rights of popular government, such as rights to freedom of speech and assembly and, by extension, to due process and equal protection of the laws. Let us call these rights to public liberties. Naturally, individuals engage in many other activities and associations in addition to those involved in the political process. Still, they are always potential participants in the discourse that governs their common life, meaning that no citizen can at any time be legitimately prevented from acting on her or his right to take part in the democratic process. Accordingly, the constitution must also stipulate certain private liberties that define each person as a member of "we the people," irrespective of whether she or he is at any given time engaged in specifically political activity. I have in mind rights to life, control of one's own body, personal property, and conscience. Were such private liberties not constitutionally protected, the political process could easily deny a person's equal standing among "we the people" by invading coercively, or permitting the coercive invasion of, her or his physical or mental capacities.[3]

---

3. Principles defining the rights to private liberties are nonetheless formative, in the sense that adherence to them is explicitly neutral to all political disagreement. Respect for private liberties only means refusal to interfere with the physical and mental capacities other individuals have – for instance, the capacity to live, to control one's

The right to freedom of religion protects, we may say, both a public and a private liberty, ensuring, on the one hand, that a person is sovereign over her or his assessment of every political claim and, on the other, that she or he has freedom of conscience throughout the full scope of her of his life. Neither the public nor the private liberties are absolute, as if the state may never constrain them in any way. But the rights in question are constitutional, meaning that the liberties of any given person are bounded only by the equal rights of all others to the same freedoms. For no other reason may constitutional freedoms be legitimately compromised by any law the state may enact, because these rights define membership in the full and free political discourse that is finally sovereign over all the laws.

If a democratic constitution must protect the public and private liberties mentioned, these rights also exhaust those properly secured by the constitution. Constitutional principles should define a state whose activities are properly determined through full and free discourse. Hence, a formative constitution, as I have called it, cannot include any stipulation of social and economic rights, such as the right to an education or to work or to health care or to a certain measure of economic resources. Although this point has been made previously, we should pause over it here. With the focus here on substantive justice, it may be more readily apparent why some will object to the limits imposed on the constitution. Membership in "we the people" is hollow, this criticism insists, without access to other conditions the community ought to provide. At the least, severe ignorance or illness or poverty effectively prevents participation in the democratic process. In addition, those enjoying unjust economic or social advantage are given, in effect, privileged entry into the political process, having more resources relevant to bending it in directions they advocate. The formative right to equal standing seems worthless and its prescription fraudulent if not combined with substantive provisions.

The objection concludes, in other words, that a strictly formative constitution is at odds with the very kind of democratic politics it seeks to establish and thus is at odds with itself. Moreover, the principle of justice as general emancipation seems to be especially solid grounds for this critique. Opportunity finds its principal source in

own body, and to decide in accord with conscience. No political question is explicitly answered by such refusal, since, in itself, it is consistent with not relating to others at all.

the community, and politically, this means general conditions of creativity provided or promoted by the state. Indeed, the ultimate terms of political assessment may be restated as a fundamental substantive right: All individuals have a right to the greatest measure of general empowerment the state can provide or promote equally for all. What is true of human achievement in all its forms holds, too, for political opportunity: Real participation requires supportive communal conditions. Those committed to the community of love, therefore, have every reason to insist that equal participation in the political process cannot be ensured by public and private liberties alone but, rather, depends also on substantive justice.

But excluding economic and social rights from constitutional stipulation does not imply that democracy can be successful without substantive justice. Insisting that all have a substantive right or set of rights the state should secure is one thing, and stipulating these rights constitutionally is something else. What justice as compound requires us to say is this: A democratic constitution *anticipates* that the full and free discourse will be successful and thus will, through statutory law, provide or promote for all the substantive conditions necessary to real equality in the political process itself. Democratic politics itself is not a substantive possibility unless the government fulfills its moral obligation by pursuing justice as general emancipation. To be sure, this obligation may not be fully met, so that we can speak of a substantively successful democracy only in the compromised sense that justice is achieved in tolerable measure. Insofar as the anticipation is unfulfilled, however, the political community is at odds with its constitution, not the constitution with itself. If the latter is democratic, it cannot guarantee success in the political process it constitutes.[4]

I suspect that some may still resist this account because they assume one or both of the following correlations: first, permanent principles belong in the constitution, and the political process properly concerns itself with changing norms for the changing circumstances of

---

4. It follows, I believe, that citizens have a moral right under certain circumstances to alter the present regime by extralegal means. When the substantive barriers to full and free discourse are sufficiently acute, the anticipation of the constitution itself permits activity that violates statutory law with a view to making the political process substantively democratic. But I will not seek here to identify the circumstances that might warrant civil disobedience or even rebellion or to specify the moral restraints on those forms of action.

the political community; second, what may finally come to the same thing, the most important things should be constitutionally guaranteed, and statutory law should be concerned with lesser matters. Hence, a strictly formative constitution implies that substantive justice has no permanent character and/or is less important. But I see no reason to accept either correlation. Because a democratic constitution presupposes the ultimate terms of political assessment, the constitution itself implies that principles of substantive justice are equally permanent, even if it does not stipulate their content. For the same reason, the constitution does not imply that statutory justice is less important. To the contrary, the entire purpose of constituting a full and free political discourse is that the substantive norms might be informed by valid principles.

The essential point, then, is that neither of the two correlations is consistent with popular sovereignty. If substantive provisions are included in the constitution, acceptance of them belongs to the ethics of citizenship, and dissent from them is not legitimate. Terms for political assessment are then stipulated by the state, and citizens are not sovereign over their assessment of every political claim. However unintentionally, those who would provide constitutional rights to economic and social conditions in fact seek to remove some understanding of substantive justice from assessment by the people and, thereby, violate their final authority.[5] In truth, substantive rights are

5. It will not help to say that constitutional provisions can themselves be assessed by the people and changed by amendment. As discussed earlier, a substantive constitutional principle requires that citizens explicitly adhere to it. The ethics of citizenship would prohibit claims for any political purpose or policy that conflicts with the principle in question, at least if one is aware of the conflict. Hence, someone who seeks to change a substantive constitutional provision would be required to accept it even while she or he does not accept it. Suppose, for instance, that the constitution stipulates in some way the principle of justice as general emancipation. Now suppose someone who rejects this principle – for instance, a free market liberal who believes that the government should restrict itself to national security, prevention of crime, enforcement of economic contracts, and other such tasks of a minimal state. This citizen would be bound to affirm justice as general emancipation even while she or he denies it. In other words, this citizen could not legitimately make a political claim for her or his assessment. The state, since it has the right to foster adherence to its constitution, would be able to teach all citizens that the principle of minimal government just suggested is wrong. Indeed, if a substantive constitutional principle does not violate popular sovereignty, there seems no reason to prohibit an established religion. Thereby, the constitution would stipulate to all citizens the ultimate terms of assessment, and no citizen could legitimately challenge them unless she or he could simultaneously believe two incompatible religions. So far as I can see, there is no way to prevent this absurdity except to insist that constitutional provisions prescribe nothing other than participation in discourse about all contested political claims.

too important to be constitutionally stipulated. No claim for any account of them should be exempt from criticism, because it cannot be valid unless it can be redeemed by the way of reason. In the end, this simply means that government by the people depends entirely on the people.

If these reflections sustain the difference and relation between formative and substantive rights, we can now confirm that Christian faith does prescribe, at least in our setting, a democratic political community. This follows because private and public liberties are themselves emancipating and, moreover, do not conflict with maximizing general empowerment. Equal rights to these liberties always enhance and never diminish the extent of general creative opportunity to which all have equal access. We may assume any measure we please of physical and psychological well-being, economic provision and opportunity, education, and so forth and suppose that these conditions are equally available to all. General emancipation can be only greater if citizens also enjoy the right to formative equality in the discourse through which justice is secured. We can also put the point this way: If we are called to empower all through and for the sake of maximal mutuality, government by the people is the indispensable political form of this pursuit. Giving to and receiving from others democratic respect as members of "we the people" is the constitutive political mutuality essential to the community of love. At least under modern conditions, our best response to God's all-embracing love includes our love for democracy at its best.

Having reached this conviction, we have also established that politics is a common Christian vocation, and the grounds for it may be summarized: The God whom Jesus decisively reveals calls every person to pursue the community of love and thus the creativity of all through and for the sake of maximal human mutuality. Justice as general emancipation is the political substance of this divine purpose and government by the people the political form of its pursuit. All Christians, in being called to serve the divine purpose, are thus called to exercise their privilege as democratic citizens for the sake of justice as general emacipation. It then follows that the early account cannot have abiding authority for Christian witness. If the political accommodation thinkers from Paul to Augustine prescribed or permitted was fitting, it was an application of the essential Christian calling to specific political circumstances – because, in our situation, that calling includes a common political vocation.

Another word should be added to clarify what this vocation does not mean. Naturally, politics is not the only form of Christian witness. Response to God's abiding call occurs within all forms of human association, including the activities of the Christian church. Any given Christian, like any human being, is faced with diverse and often competitive demands and opportunities and is typically required to choose how, given her or his circumstances, time and talents are best allocated. The inclusive divine purpose cannot itself dictate those decisions. Hence, nothing we have established here determines the relative priorities of political activity and other practices in the life of any given Christian or group of Christians. Speaking of some Christian vocation as common simply marks it as inseparable from the calling to Christian faith itself, in distinction from a specialized calling to some occupation or profession, secular or religious, that properly belongs only to some Christians.

Each common Christian vocation, then, defines a witness that should typically be included in every Christian life, although exceptions are always possible. At the least, any common form of witness is persistently among the demands and opportunities any given Christian will recognize as competitive for her or his specific purposes. Under modern conditions that are or approach being democratic, politics is such a vocation. Moreover, the grounds for this conclusion also provide the terms in which Christians should assess the relative importance of this calling. For most early Christian thinkers, as we have seen, the principal context of moral concern was properly the Christian church itself, in which the new life of Christian faith found social expression. However justified in their circumstances these early thinkers may have been, the abiding content of Christian faith is so far from implying this focus as to direct Christian commitment toward maximal mutuality within the encompassing human community. In this light, the measure of empowerment provided by our wider social structure has its own profound significance, because the general order politics provides or promotes affects for good or ill the potential for all other forms of mutuality. The principle of justice as general emancipation, we can say, was implicit when our earlier discussion took for granted the profound consequences of political rule for worldly good and evil. Those consequences become the more worthy of a

Christian's attention today when, by that principle, they fall far short, and I will suggest in the next two chapters that Christians in the United States face this challenge.

III   THE ULTIMATE GROUND OF WORTH

Christians who embrace popular sovereignty because they seek to love all that God loves thereby also concede that their principle of justice may itself be contested in the democratic discourse, which does or can stretch to claims for ultimate terms of political assessment. To affirm justice as general emancipation is also to allow that here, too, is a political claim over which the people have political authority. But this concession does not put Christians at odds with themselves, because their faith also commits them to the way of reason. They are bound by their own principle to agree that political decisions should *not* be controlled by it unless it can be validated by argument. Still, Christians do claim validity for their belief that God's all-embracing love is the ultimate ground of worth and, thereby, pledge that prescribing the community of love can be redeemed in full and free political discourse.

The overall purpose of this work requires at least some comment on how this pledge can be carried through. If it cannot, then democratic politics as a *Christian* vocation will finally be incoherent. Address to this concern is the more imperative because we previously underscored that most thinkers within the Christian tradition have denied argumentative validation of Christian belief and because, we noted, this view of their faith is still widely shared by contemporary Christians. The attempt here to chart a different course will be aided by a brief return to that earlier discussion.

Seeking to show why Christians today may affirm the way of reason, we saw that fidelity to their tradition compels some explanation of its majority voice, which has, beginning with early explications of Christian faith, taken a different position. In an effort to suggest how that explanation might proceed, we considered the conceptual context indebted to Greek metaphysics, and I proposed the following: Summarily speaking, the basic assumptions of this legacy became so controlling of theological reflection that alternatives to them did not come into view. None of these assumptions was more fundamental

than the idea of change or the capacity to change as the mark of imperfection. It then followed that God as the perfect source and end of
all things must be completely changeless and thus completely nontemporal or eternal. So understood, God can be designated in literal
terms only by negation, as the theological tradition has largely asserted, and a divine nature to which no positive terms literally apply
cannot be demonstrated by natural reason. Given their attempt to
explicate Christian theism within this framework, Christian thinkers
could justifiably conclude that this belief cannot be redeemed, at least
not fully redeemed, by argument.

If this reading is correct, the humanistic commitment implies that
Christian faith cannot be true unless the God it affirms is not completely changeless or eternal. This means that Christians who affirm
the way of reason cannot redeem their theistic belief unless another
conception of God is both possible and, at least in our context, more
appropriate to the abiding content of Christian faith. Absent that alternative, the principles of justice grounded in God's call cannot be
validated in discourse, and democratic politics as a Christian vocation will finally be incoherent. Hence, the overall purpose of this work
requires some reason to think that contemporary Christians need not
accept the conception of God's nature that has so dominated the tradition they inherit. If this demand can be met, we might thereby also
suggest that justice as general emancipation not only implies a democratic political community but also should control the activities of
the state.

A more adequate conception of the God Christians affirm is, I believe, available and can be approached through further reflection on
God's all-embracing love. Loving others, we have said, is giving of
oneself in a manner that seeks their own good, and thus God calls us
to love one another because God's love wills our good or the flourishing of all. It is pertinent now to recall that God directs us to this
community of love because living with this purpose is implied by the
first and most fundamental commandment: "You shall love the Lord
your God with all your heart, and with all your soul, and with all
your mind, and with all your strength" (Mark 12: 30). We are to love
all that God loves because we are to love God without reservation.
But if this is the meaning of Christian faith, we are bound to infer that
its God not only loves but also wills to be loved and thus not only
gives to us but also receives from us. Although receiving from and

giving to God must be essentially different from human mutuality, the abiding content of Christian faith leads us nonetheless to speak of a unique mutuality between ourselves and the divine source and end of all things.

That affirmation of divine–human mutuality is, to the best of my reasoning, inconsistent with the traditional conception of God as completely changeless. Our love for God can be expressed only through the decisions we make in the course of our lives or through our creative activities, in each of which we change ourselves and the wider world by adding to the world a new moment of human achievement. Thus, the divine reality can be a recipient of our love only if it, too, is subject to change. Moreover, change and temporality imply each other, as Augustine rightly said. "Without motion and change there is no time, while in eternity there is no change" (1984: 435). Hence, the God whom we are called to love without reservation cannot be completely eternal and must be, in God's own eminent or perfect way, a temporal reality.

To assert a divine or perfect form of change and temporality is, naturally, to depart from the classical Greek view of change or the capacity to change as a mark of imperfection. But there is no reason to resist that departure. Indeed, reflection on ourselves in distinction from other creatures we experience shows that our life with understanding is especially important precisely because it enjoys a greater capacity for change. The lifeless things of the world are those that most approach being changeless through the course of their existence. Plants grow and bloom, but the scope of their change is confined to a particular place and, with relatively minor if sometimes fascinating variations, is largely the same for all members of the same species. Nonhuman animals enjoy possibilities for movement and other more extensive forms of alteration, but here changes are largely confined by instinct and, with the possible exception of a few species, include no capacity for self-conscious decision. When we reach human existence, "the Rubicon has been crossed" (Whitehead 1938: 38). Comparatively speaking, life with understanding includes dramatic capacities to introduce something new and to alter both oneself and the world. For this reason, we can speak in an emphatic sense of humans as distinctive and creative individuals.

The recognition that higher kinds of creatures are those with greater openness to change at least suggests that imperfection is not properly measured thereby. To the contrary, a perfect or divine reality would seem, by extension of the reasoning, to have this capacity in a way that cannot be rivaled, so that God is the reality supremely subject to change. Among twentieth-century attempts to explicate Christian faith, conceptions of God as the eminent subject of change were developed most clearly by theologians who appropriate the metaphysical formulations of Alfred North Whitehead and Charles Hartshorne.[6] Roughly speaking, this alternative metaphysics occupies in the thought of these theologians the place filled in so much of the Christian tradition by the fundamental assumptions of classical Greek philosophy.

Naturally, theologians indebted to this alternative differ, just as thinkers indebted to classical Greek assumptions have disagreed with each other. Still, the "neoclassical" conception of God, as it is sometimes called, may be summarized here in a manner that will serve our purposes. The divine reality is the universal or perfect individual, and God's character may be clarified by marking its similarity to and difference from the nature of a human person. In earlier discussion, we described a distinctively human life as a course or career of activities. Each activity begins with experience of the past, both the individual's own past and the wider nonhuman and human contexts, and completes itself by its decision, through which the received past is unified and the present activity makes a difference to the future. A good or flourishing life, we continued, requires emancipation, meaning that one's course of activities includes increasing potential for creativity, and the good in this sense depends on the particular past each given activity inherits. We can now add that human possibilities, however emancipated or profound they may become, are limited in principle because our relations to the past are always fragmentary. While we exhibit a striking capacity to carry what we have been and done into the present, even our memory is partial, and, for all its richness, our experience of the wider world and the lives of other humans can include but a small fragment of the immensity beyond us.

On neoclassical theism, it is this fragmentariness that marks our difference from God. Hence, the perfect or divine reality is like each of us as an individual existing by way of successive activities, but

---

6. For their most systematic statements, see Whitehead 1978; Hartshorne 1970. For briefer statements, see Whitehead 1938: chap. 6; Hartshorne 1967.

different from all others because each of its experiences includes without loss all of the past. Everything that has ever happened in all of its detail is something a divine activity receives, so that God in the present moment unifies strictly comprehensive appreciation. Indeed, we can define the past in its entirety as whatever past is presently experienced by God. The universal individual is at any given moment the unified whole of all that has been and the individual who will, in subsequent activities, add to this totality whatever occurs in the future as and when it occurs. So far from being completely changeless, then, God is the eminent subject of change because God always has been and always will be the sole individual who receives and, thereby, is changed by strictly everything else as it makes its appearance in the world.

To be sure, there is one kind of change to which we are, in a sense, subject and God is not. "All people are grass, their constancy is like the flower of the field. . . . The grass withers, the flower fades; but the word of our God will stand for ever" (Isaiah 40:6–8). As the ultimate source and end of all things, the divine individual cannot come into being or cease to be. In contrast, our fragmentary lives enjoy a measured span of years; we are born and we die. But these are not really changes *in* us; they are, rather, changes in the world or, better, changes in the abiding experience of God. Unlike all others, the divine individual is supremely temporal, a course of universal activities without beginning or ending that again and again includes whatever else there is and thus time and again brings to supreme unity whatever world there may be.

I submit that this view, when compared to the idea dominating prior Christian thought, provides Christians more appropriate terms for understanding the God they find in their experience of Jesus, the ultimate ground of worth whose love commands unreserved love for God and all the world. Our authenticity is achieved by decision for this self-understanding because God is the individual by whom everything we become in all of its detail is received, and what we do should be done for all the world because the world in all of its detail is likewise received by the divine life. Loving the world *is* loving God, in the sense that God's love receives all the world. We are called to love our neighbors as ourselves because thereby we contribute most fully to the divine good, and that is why the second part of the Great Commandment follows without pause from the first.

In contrast, to understand God as eternally complete is finally to deny any ultimate importance to what we do or become. Whatever effect we have in the world, we cannot make a difference to something that cannot receive it. Perhaps more than anything else, that implication is the most compelling indictment of theism indebted to the classical Greek assumption. Still, the point is not simply that we are left without ultimate worth, if this is taken to say that life would still have whatever importance it has for others in the world. To the contrary, Christian faith asserts that God as all-embracing love is the ground of all worth. The effects we have in the world would be without any worth except that the world has the significance God gives to it by receiving all of it into the everlasting divine life. In the end, the only difference we can make is the difference we make to the divine good.

If an extended discussion would sustain this reading as the meaning of Christian faith, perhaps Christian belief in God can also be fully validated by the way of reason. At the least, doubt or denial of this possibility on the grounds that God must be completely eternal and thus, by implication, can be designated literally only by negation is no longer pertinent. We can now understand perfection in terms both literal and positive: God is the universal and eminently temporal individual that unifies again and again the whole of which everything else is or becomes a part. Thereby, a long-standing deterrent to knowledge of God through convincing argument is removed.

Given only what has been said, moreover, we can offer reasons authorized by common human experience through which to warrant belief in this God. The argument proceeds from our nature as creatures who live with understanding and, therefore, decide in each present moment by evaluating as better or worse the alternatives for purpose given to us. Given this essential condition, we could not be human at all without affirming that our decisions make a difference. Consciously to choose a purpose *is* to claim significance for one's life because one decides for something taken to be good. Since that belief is inescapable, we cannot consistently take as true anything inconsistent with it. But, now, it does seem inconsistent to say that what we become could have significance without making an ultimate difference. Were there nothing ultimate at stake in what we do, then ultimately there would be nothing at stake. We who choose among our specific possibilities by taking some purpose to be good cannot sensibly believe that this purpose finally has no point at all. So far as I can see, it is finally impossible to understand ourselves in terms of a final nullity, as if our lives were only a brief flicker of light with only darkness before and darkness after. "It haunts our imagination," Whitehead wrote, "that the immediate facts of present action pass into permanent significance for the universe. The insistent notions of Right and Wrong, Achievement and Failure, depend upon this background. Otherwise, every activity is merely a passing whiff of insignificance" (1941: 698). But if this is so, there must be some everlasting reality to which human life makes a difference, and that conclusion points the way toward an all-embracing or all-loving divine individual.[7]

A thorough case for the credibility of Christian faith is beyond the proper scope of the present work. But perhaps enough has been said to encourage confidence that making this case is not the transparently impossible task it is so widely assumed to be. Thereby, Christians might be led to claim validity for their conviction of faith within the democratic discourse – and thus to advocate the community of love as the substantive ideal by which democracy is grounded and to which activities of the democratic state should be directed.

---

7. Even if they concede that belief in an all-embracing reality is implied, some will object that this argument fails to establish the reality of God. What humans must believe is one thing, this objection holds, and what is true is another. Perhaps humans inescapably claim significance for their lives and, therefore, must also believe that there is an all-embracing reality to which they make a difference. Nonetheless, this says something only about humans, and it remains that their inescapable belief may be false because there is no such reality. I do not find this objection convincing. To assert that our necessary affirmation of God may be nonetheless false is to say that *this* assertion can be believed. In fact, however, anyone who believes it does so inconsistently. She or he simultaneously claims validity for "There is an all-embracing reality," since believing this is inescapable, and for "There may not be an all-embracing reality" – and thereby says, in effect, "I believe X, and I do not believe X." So far as I can see, a belief without which we could not understand or believe anything at all must be true. The discussion in this section is indebted to Ogden 1966: 1–70.

Chapter 5

Religious Decisions at Stake

Christian faith prescribes, at least in our setting, a democratic political community. Our journey to this conclusion has been extended because full clarity about the prescription involves understandings of democracy and Christian faith that are, in some respects, contrary to widespread opinion. A democratic constitution defines politics as government through full and free discourse and, therefore, requires that religious convictions can be validated and invalidated by argument. The way of reason is also prescribed by Christian faith. It claims to represent the authenticity for which every human can decide and, thereby, affirms that its own abiding content can be assessed through reasons authorized by common human experience. Moreover, the substantive principles of Christian faith prescribe democracy because government by the people is essential to the community of love, to which God's call directs all human purposes. Thus, the life of Christian witness includes a common political vocation aimed at maximizing the access to general conditions of creativity that is equally available to all.

I THE AIM AT JUSTICE

The importance of this vocation is worth underscoring. Human mutuality is the principal worldly source of the good life God wills for all, and the communal conditions of creativity stretch from our most personal and intimate relationships through neighborhoods, voluntary associations, and institutions of work and culture to the general character or structures of the political community as a whole. Activities

of state govern the general context in which all life with others occurs, and the possibilities delivered to individuals by their more specific associations, including their personal relationships, are severely
debased by injustice. If the state does not provide or promote the
requisite equal access to physical safety, health care, economic provision, significant work, education, patterns of enriching association,
and the like, other associations within the community typically cannot overcome the creative opportunities lost to most who suffer the
political failure. The consequences are, perhaps, even more obvious
when the state supports or permits institutional forms of racial or
sexual abasement or when covert forms of inequality violate rights
to public and private liberties, for instance, through corruption in the
criminal justice system.

We might reformulate the basic point this way: The wider political
order ought to provide or promote general conditions for local associations to provide or promote specific conditions so that, through
both, the empowerment of all is maximized. Thereby, our life together
becomes a mosaic of associations so fitted as to maximize mutuality.
Since the general pattern sets the indispensable context for distinctive
achievement by each part, justice as general emancipation is essential to the community of love, and politics is a common Christian
vocation.

With this accounting, we can avoid both sides of a conflict that often divided the Christian community during the twentieth century.
On one side, many seemed to separate the life of faith from politics.
For those so aligned, the message entrusted to the church concerns
ultimate matters, in contrast to the transient political conditions of
this world, and attention to the latter compromises clear focus on
the former. This separation occurred not only in some expressions
of Christian fundamentalism and other conservative churches but
also in congregations typically considered more liberal theologically,
especially those whose members were economically and socially advantaged. We need not pursue a more nuanced reading of this view
or the grounds for it. The important note is that some Christians were
the more driven to "privatize" their faith because others seemed to
"politicize" theirs. Some, although not all, expressions of the social
gospel, of Christian witness during the turbulent 1960s, and of so-
called liberation theology appeared to equate the life of faith with
commitment to certain movements for social change – or, at least, to

suggest that such participation is the paramount work of Christian witness. Again, there is surely room for a more nuanced reading. Nonetheless, it is likely that advocates on this side were the more driven to less circumspect statements because those on the other side seemed to exclude political purposes from the meaning of Christian faith.

The conclusion we have reached offers a third alternative. There can be no appropriate separation of Christian witness from politics, because the community of love necessarily includes justice. At the same time, this community is far from exhausted by the general order provided and promoted by the political process. To the contrary, creative opportunity depends on all forms or occasions of human interaction. Hence, they all properly contribute to the mosaic of mutuality that should direct all our purposes. If, with Reinhold Niebuhr, "the highest reaches of . . . individuality are dependent upon the social substance out of which they arise and they must find their end and fulfillment in the community" (1944: 48), "community" does not mean solely the political order but, rather, all aspects of our life with others. As mentioned previously, politics is not the only and may not be the paramount kind of work to which a given Christian is called. She or he will have one or more specific Christian vocations within one or more nonpolitical communities – as, for instance, parent, craftsperson, artist, nurse, educator, or preacher. Further, politics is not the only and, perhaps, not the paramount vocation common to all Christians. But it is essential to the life of contemporary Christian witness, because democratic justice is essential to the community of love.

We can also avoid another misguided kind of conflict having an extended history among American Christians and especially evident in recent decades. This division is found among some who agree that Christians are called to a political witness but disagree about the particular governmental activities to be advocated. On political issues ranging from New Deal economic regulation to entry into World War II to engagement in Vietnam to affirmative action, welfare policy, environmental protection, the character of public education, the relation of local government to federal institutions, and the national response to international terrorism, the larger Christian community has reached diverse assessments. In itself, however, such political diversity is not the misguided discord I have in mind. The latter occurs when differing positions on some particular public issue are thought by their respective advocates to be religious differences, in the sense that Christians could not really disagree politically if they all properly understood the abiding content of their faith. A particular political purpose or agenda then becomes a tenet of Christian faith or defines proper participation in the Christian community. Particular political disagreements are treated as if they were about the Christian confession, and each side declares that the other is deficiently Christian or heretical.

Against any such charge, the common political vocation defined by our reflections does not itself dictate any agenda of public purposes beyond the pursuit of justice as general emancipation. The abiding content of Christian faith answers the abiding human question about life's ultimate worth, naming as our ultimate source and end the God revealed through Jesus Christ, so that human authenticity is unreserved love for this God and, thereby, unreserved commitment to the community of love. This answer gives Christians ultimate or most general terms of political evaluation, articulated in the principle or principles of justice implied by their commitment. In contrast, decisions about issues such as those mentioned in the previous paragraph are particular political assessments, which are reached only by applying the ultimate or general terms to particular circumstances. The principles of justice do not apply themselves. Fitting resolution of any specific issue waits further on judgments about the particular facts of the given situation.

For Christians, we might say, the community of love and its principles of justice define the grand design of our common adventure, rather like the design given to an epic novel by the author's comprehensive point. In contrast, particular political issues concern details of the community, corresponding to the diverse events through whose narration the epic point is made. Just as an author's clarity about her or his basic purpose does not determine which characters or events will best serve it, so particular assessments cannot be derived directly from the general purpose of our common life. Reaching those decisions requires judgments about states of affairs in which one seeks details that best fit with the grand design or exemplify the principles of justice. In a word, particular political conclusions require an exercise of practical reason or Christian praxis. On Aristotle's classic account, practical wisdom is summarily described as deliberation through which a universal rule of good action is applied to a given decision by way of judgments about the particular situation. Similarly, the principles of justice as general emancipation cannot be deliberately exemplified without knowledge of the detailed circumstances in which a specific issue arises and must be resolved.

It follows that Christians who share a clear and appropriate account of their faith and do their best to reach political assessments consistent with it may nonetheless disagree about given political issues. To be sure, such discord among Christians, as among citizens generally, may result from the bias one or more of the parties allow their more narrow interests to introduce, so that particular conclusions are in fact informed by some distortion of the general principles to which persons purport to be committed. Quite apart from invasion by that common human fault, however, disagreement may be occasioned by differing views of the relevant circumstances to which Christians seek to apply a shared understanding of justice. The latter possibility becomes more apparent when we observe that circumstances relevant to important political decisions can be immensely complex, so that appreciation of them by any given individual is likely to be in consequential respects incomplete.

This does not imply that Christians who, sharing appropriate principles of justice, reach differing particular assessments about, say, affirmative action or tax proposals or foreign policy are equally right or equally fitting in their witness. To the contrary, one party to the disagreement may well be more accurate in reading the relevant circumstances and more accomplished in the kind of deliberation through which principles are applied. Accordingly, one response to the particular issue at hand may be, or may more fully approach, an adequate application of the general principles commonly affirmed. As a democratic citizen, therefore, each Christian is bound to seek as best she or he can, perhaps through the kind of discourse with other Christians in which faulty or fragmentary purchase on the relevant facts is corrected or improved, proper political application and, if necessary and insofar as she or he is able, to argue for it. The point here is simply that dissonant conclusions may result from disparity in the more particular judgments required, and, when this occurs, disagreement among Christians is not a difference about the content of their faith. In sum, beliefs that characterize the Christian confession are one thing, and particular political assessments are another, however fundamental the former are to all who practice politics as a common Christian vocation.

Once we stress this difference, some might propose that democratic commitment is itself a particular political assessment. On this view, we erred in saying that democratic principles of justice are included in or implied by the essential meaning of Christian faith. To the contrary, they can be reached only as an application of Christian belief to special circumstances. Indeed, we might be told, this reading is simply an inference from our own previous discussion. The application of Christian faith to specific circumstances became important when we asked whether the early account of political responsibility is authoritative for contemporary Christians. That account, I have argued, was an application of Christian faith to a political situation in which rule by the many was neither a present nor, perhaps, a foreseeable possibility. In a similar way, some may now conclude, democratic commitment specifies Christian faith to the modern political situation, thereby illustrating the difference between essential content and particular political decisions. Hence, Christians who share a clear and appropriate understanding of their faith may nonetheless disagree about the prescription of democracy and, with it, the definition of justice as general emancipation.

But this line of reasoning is, I believe, misleading. The political responsibilities prescribed by early Christian thinkers can now be seen as a specification of Christian faith precisely because modernity has opened the possibility neither present nor, perhaps, foreseeable during the early centuries of the Christian community. Given that rule by the many is now among the alternatives, the essential Christian calling to love God and, therefore, all others without reservation implies a democratic commitment. Hence, this commitment "applies" the Christian faith to modern political circumstances only in the sense that democracy cannot be prescribed if it cannot occur. In other words, Christians in our situation consistently reject this prescription only if they mean to say that popular sovereignty is not a real alternative. But this does not make democratic commitment and, therefore, justice as general emancipation a particular political assessment of the kind we previously discussed. Particular judgments in that sense involve laws or policies or actions about which disagreement may arise because one must decide between real possibilities. What becomes contested because Christian principles must be applied is not whether one or another political course can occur but, rather, which among the real alternatives should be chosen.

Given only that government by the people is a real possibility, then, the abiding content of Christian faith prescribes it. To be sure, some contemporary Christians who concede its possibility might nonetheless reject democracy or, more likely, contest the principles of justice as general emancipation. But this disagreement concerns the content of Christian faith itself, what it includes or implies, and thus the reading of it given in this work. If we take that reading to be appropriate, moreover, contemporary Christians might even say that the early account applied to its situation a democratic ideal shared by all Christians across the centuries – meaning thereby the following: In earlier centuries, accommodation to the one or the few was a proper way to pursue long-run conditions under which rule by the many might occur, even if Paul or Augustine or other early Christians could not have thought about the matter in this way. Christians today, therefore, should distinguish their essential commitment to this democratic ideal from particular political assessments in which the principles of justice as general emancipation are applied.

Commending this distinction does not deny that disagreements over particular issues may more or less transparently betray differences about the essence of Christian faith or the principles implied by it. This is so when the relevant circumstances are themselves more or less transparent, and there is no real possibility of differing assessments based on differing judgments about particular states of affairs. The moral conflict over slavery that divided American Christians prior to and during the Civil War is an especially clear illustration. Those who defended the "peculiar institution" could do so only from ultimate terms of assessment profoundly in opposition to the community of love. We merely restate the point in noting that slavery is a transparent violation of the rights to public and private liberties defining all who are ruled as members of "we the people." If the Christian faith prescribes democracy, it prescribes the formative principles of a democratic constitution. Hence, a political assertion that transparently violates those principles must express a denial of the faith they articulate.

When political disagreements of this kind occur, Christians have good cause to see their discord as inherently religious and thus to plead that others misrepresent the faith they claim to confess.

Discourse among Christians is then properly focused on the abiding content of their common calling. The conflict Christians since the Civil War have experienced with respect to racism is or includes, I expect, a further case in point, and there may also be others. Wherever it is fitting, however, the conclusion that Christians who disagree politically must also disagree religiously requires that differing estimates of the relevant particular circumstances are not really possible. So stating the matter preserves the distinction between beliefs essential to the Christian confession and particular political assessments, because we imply that the former must be applied to reach the latter, even while saying that, with respect to some political decisions, the application may be transparent. At the same time, then, we underscore that Christians who do not disagree about the meaning of their faith may well reach differing political assessments when the relevant judgments about given states of affairs are not obvious.

II ALTERNATIVE IDEALS FOR COMMUNITY

Given the distinction we have just been at some pains to draw, a general explication of politics as a Christian vocation cannot include specific conclusions about particular contemporary issues. The latter depend on current circumstances, judgments about which are not contained in or implied by the Christian confession. In the rest of this work, I will seek to illustrate the importance of Christian faith and its principles of justice to contemporary United States politics. But these discussions will include readings of relevant states of affairs from which other Christians may dissent, and this is the point in speaking of illustrations. Other views of the circumstances might lead to differing outcomes. Still, showing why other conclusions require contrary judgments about our situation confirms that commitment to the community of love makes a difference for decisions "we the people" must take. Moreover, I am persuaded that my own readings are substantially correct, so that, secondarily, I seek to commend the political conclusions.

The next chapter will consider three specific political issues. This chapter seeks to identify fundamental disagreements that I take to be widely implicated in American politics and consequential in shaping the specific issues treated subsequently. Even here, however, particular judgments of a kind are unavoidable. One cannot disclose such basic differences without interpreting the commitments informing differing individuals and groups, and the persuasions of one's fellow citizens are, in their own way, among the particularities of our contemporary public life. Even the fundamental disagreements presently influential are, in other words, among the relevant circumstances of our political situation. Here too, then, I recognize that some who substantially accept the principles of justice we have articulated may offer differing conclusions about the political task we are given – although, again, I do mean to commend the reading I offer.

In preparation, we should emphasize a fact about our political life that has been central throughout our discussion of democracy, namely, that politics is related inescapably to implicit or explicit convictions about the ultimate terms of political assessment. For Christians, this is because all humans live by way of a primal decision for or against the God of all-embracing love. But whether or not the Christian faith is true, it remains that every political claim implies some or other principle or principles for evaluating all actual and proposed activities of the state. Even if someone holds that principles of justice are independent of any conception of the comprehensive good, or that no such principles prescribe for politics universally, she or he cannot make a claim for the justice of any political decision without implying an understanding of ultimate terms for this assessment. We may also say that she or he implicitly affirms some understanding of the ultimate ground of worth, namely, whatever it is that authorizes those ultimate terms. In this extended sense, all political claims imply an understanding of the inclusive purpose of human life, even if one explicitly denies that there is a single purpose and affirms only a plurality of proper aims, each of which is specific to a given realm of life or to a given community.

This, we may recall, is the extended meaning of "religious" proper to the meaning of religious freedom as a democratic principle, because every conviction about the ultimate terms of political assessment is, in its own way, an answer to the question the state may not explicitly address without violating popular sovereignty (see Chapter 2, Section II). With a view to the possibility that any such answer can become the object of discussion and debate, we can say that religious convictions are always implicated in politics. On this accounting, something is awry in recent discussions, which have attained some prominence in both the academy and the larger public discourse, about *whether* it is legitimate or, at least, prudent to allow religious claims within the political process. So formulating the question implies that religious convictions might be kept separate from politics. But this is impossible if every claim for ultimate terms for political assessment is, in the sense proper to government by the people, religious.

Since ultimate terms for political assessment are always involved, disagreement or contention about some particular political issue may include, even if the participants are not mindful of them, differing religious convictions. I do not suggest that all political conflict is based on religious differences. We have already seen that Christians who share a clear and appropriate understanding of their faith may nonetheless reach conflicting political conclusions by virtue of differing judgments about particular circumstances. Similarly, disagreement in the wider democratic discourse may occur among citizens who agree in substance about general terms of assessment but have divergent readings of the relevant state of affairs. Still, discord between or among convictions protected by religious freedom is always possible, and political disagreement that is more or less fundamental likely implicates differing ultimate terms of assessment. Whenever this is the case, a religious decision is at stake in our public life.

Saying this does not mean that democratic procedures should reach an explicit verdict about which of the contending religious convictions is true – as if the institutions through which activities of state are determined must include, say, a vote among the people or among their representatives through which a common decision about our inclusive purpose is explicitly reached. Any such procedure would obviously violate the prohibition of religious establishment, since the result would be an official religious conviction. Religious freedom limits the official decision-making procedure and thus the activities of state to more or less specialized political assessments or specialized norms of order to be enforced throughout the political community – for instance, norms that define criminal activity and valid contracts, regulate economic activity, prohibit discrimination, provide educational opportunity, control treatment of the natural environment, relate the nation to the larger community of nations, and so forth. Nonetheless, any such decision will *imply* an understanding of the community's inclusive purpose or the ultimate terms of political assessment. Thus, when democratic discourse involves alternatives for legislation or policy based on differing beliefs about those terms, the official course taken cannot avoid *implicitly* taking sides in a religious disagreement. This is the sense in which a religious decision may be at stake in our political life.

It also follows, then, that *explicit* attention to politically relevant religious differences belongs entirely to discussion and debate among "we the people," in distinction from the activities of state they determine. Among the people, it is entirely proper and often pressing that contending accounts of the community's inclusive purpose should be deliberately advocated, criticized, and defended. Thereby, citizens and their representatives, as they engage in the official decision-making procedure, might choose specialized norms in light of the most convincing ultimate terms of assessment. Perhaps, as some have observed, discourse about religious claims typically occurs best outside more official institutions of political decision making – for instance, legislatures or courts or political caucuses and campaigns. For the most part, the media, civic associations, educational institutions, and the like may, by virtue of their distance from immediate particular decisions, facilitate more readily common reflection on more inclusive beliefs about the public purpose (see Hollenbach: 165f.). In addition, formal institutions of political rule are, perhaps, more easily dominated by terms of assessment that become highly resistant to fundamental challenge, so that a vital informal realm of political discourse is typically indispensable (see Dryzek: chap. 4). Still, there is no way in principle to restrict the settings proper to religious debate, since the judgment about which claims are relevant on what occasions is itself one that properly belongs to each democratic citizen as she or he participates in the political process. In any event, that debate is essential to democratic politics. Government by the people prohibits an official answer to the religious question in order that decisions of the political community may conform as fully as possible with the answer full and free discourse can redeem.

Those who pursue politics as a Christian vocation intend to apply an explicit view of our inclusive purpose and the ultimate ground of worth by which it is authorized. Hence, they have special reason to ask about and, where needed, call attention to religious decisions at stake in public life, and I propose now to illustrate how such decisions are present. As we focus in this way, let us recall that alternative religious convictions implicitly or explicitly involved in political dis-agreement need not be those of commonly recognized religious tra-ditions, such as Christianity or Islam or Judaism, or of communi-ties that embody differing expressions of such traditions. Within the democratic process, a religious conviction is any formulation of the inclusive purpose or the ultimate terms of assessment. Thus, a given conviction of this kind may not include a belief in some transcendent reality on which all of the world somehow depends. In the sense rel-evant here, a religious orientation may be throughly this-worldly or secularistic, whereby the worth of life is not ultimately grounded by anything other than the human adventure itself or the larger realm of worldly things. What I will now offer is a general reading of con-temporary United States politics in order to suggest how Christians today might consider their political vocation in relation to religious issues that "we the people" must somehow or other resolve.

Having identified this vocation by way of the community of love, we can clarify the relevant religious issues by asking whether and, if so, what alternative ideals for community are effective in our con-temporary public life For its adherents, an ideal of this kind defines the community's inclusive purpose and thus belongs to some belief about the ultimate ground of worth. I will summarize two communal ideals that are contrary to Christian commitment and, on my account-ing, are pervasive in contemporary political opinion. Their influence does not require that citizens moved by them are reflective about this effect. As often as not, I expect, ideals are received and accepted as a part of some cultural legacy and subsequently guide specific judg-ments without being examined or even consciously delineated, and the two I will discuss both have, on my reading, a deep background in American history. They are here portrayed as something like what Max Weber, in another use of the term, called "ideal types." For the sake of clarity, in other words, these inclusive communal designs will be displayed in sharp contrasts. Perhaps political participants rarely adhere without qualification to one or the other, and thus they appear in public only with greater or lesser purity. On my reading, they are nonetheless widely consequential.

I will call these rivals to the community of love the "liberal" and "conservative" ideals of community. These terms are used in varying ways by differing political theorists, and, in some plausible sense of each term, one might effectively argue that all or most Americans are liberals, even while they are also conservatives. I will not pursue the diversity of meanings found in the theoretical discussion. For present purposes, the more relevant comment is that these terms are also common currency in contemporary public discussion. Noting this is useful because, using "liberal" and "conservative" as names for communal ideals, I intend somewhat different meanings than the terms often assume in the wider political discourse, and the contrast with their usage there will help to present what I have in mind.

Roughly speaking, "conservative" in its more familiar sense names the general commitment to minimizing governmental activity and maximizing individual liberty or freedom from interference, and this view is sometimes also called libertarian. In distinction, "liberal" commonly means the general belief that prescribes for the state a more extensive responsibility, especially toward securing for all a basic level of conditions prerequisite to well-being, and liberals in this sense are sometimes said to advocate the welfare state. But the disagreements between these two political orientations, although often of moment, may also be understood as a family quarrel because, at a deeper level, libertarians and welfare liberals typically share or encourage the same ideal for community. For both, the inclusive public purpose is to serve, subject to constraints of national defense and certain equal rights, the satisfaction of private interests or the fulfillment of private ends. As I intend the term, the "liberal ideal" is defined by this encompassing design.

So understood, liberals believe that individual decision should determine for each person the substance of a good life. Community is, consequently, instrumental to interests, and its proper function is independent of any given one. This is the sense in which the ends are private. To be sure, a given individual may have an interest in communal participation, including political participation. But this interest is seen as another private end. Hence, it becomes one among the many diverse aims diverse individuals choose and to which the larger community is instrumental. Since the flourishing of any given person is defined by her or his own decision, the point of our common life is to provide, subject to constraints of national defense and certain equal rights, certain conditions or resources useful to all pursuits individuals elect or happen to prefer.

For this reason, the liberal ideal historically has forged an alliance with the modern economic order. Economic activity is or can be organized to produce and distribute goods and services as means to want-satisfaction or "consumer preferences." Although we should not speak of strict entailment, the conception of community as servant to private ends leads easily to the view that our social order is better insofar as it provides, within the constraints mentioned, more instrumental resources, and the obvious measure of greater or lesser resources in this sense is economic. When this alliance informs political expression of the liberal ideal, advocates typically urge that economic goals and processes should be supreme within the social order, and the community's inclusive purpose is, given national security and fairness, to maximize want-satisfaction by maximizing economic prosperity and growth. Many have argued that something very like this bearing has dominated our national life since the Union prevailed in the Civil War, setting the stage for dramatic industrial development in the later nineteenth century. I, too, believe that liberalism in this economic expression has been and continues to be profoundly effective in our public life, and I will henceforth focus attention on the liberal ideal in this form.[1]

Because they share this communal ideal, libertarian and welfare liberals find their principal disagreements focused on how economic

1. In order to avoid misunderstanding, I stress that my characterization of liberalism is not one to which all political theorists who consider themselves liberal would consent. For one thing, the term "liberal" is sometimes used broadly to mean simply the affirmation of individual liberties in the sense I have explicated as a set of formative rights. In this sense, democracy as government by the people is inherently liberal, and those who affirm political principles derived from the pursuit of maximal mutuality are themselves liberals. We inherit an especially clear instance of the latter in the reconstructed liberalism of John Dewey (see Dewey). More commonly, I expect, "liberal" is currently taken to designate those for whom politics is instrumental to diverse ends. But some who so affirm distinguish between ends whose overall attainment can be maximized and conceptions of the good from which principles of justice should be separated, holding that maximal want-satisfaction is simply one inclusive conception of value (see, e.g., Barry, Larmore, Rawls 1996, Galston). Further, some who affirm maximal want-satisfaction may reject the idea that greater or lesser success in this purpose can be measured by traditional economic calculations.

Among thinkers who separate justice from inclusive conceptions of value, there are also different conceptions of justice, some of which are not those of libertarians or welfare liberals, as I have portrayed these alternatives. One of these, John Rawls's general conception of justice, was especially important to the formulation of justice as general emancipation in Chapter 4 (see Chapter 4, fn. 2). But the differences among liberal proposals of this kind cannot, on my accounting, finally be adjudicated because valid principles of justice cannot be separated from the comprehensive good. Hence, every proposed separation implies its own conception of that good, and I have argued for this theoretical conclusion elsewhere (see Gamwell 2000: chap. 5). For all that, however, my focus here is not the theoretical discussion of liberalism and its meanings. Rather, I seek to designate an ideal for community that is, on my reading, pervasively effective in our public life.

resources should be distributed. For libertarians, government should in the main refrain from changing the distribution effected through the free market. Such interference, sometimes said to be inherently wrong, is at least misguided, because it weakens personal incentives to be productive and thus reduces overall economic growth. For welfare liberals, the free market distribution is unreliable, and other forces, especially government, must modify the outcome to ensure that basic needs are met and that all have the economic prerequisites of opportunity. In either case, however, social and political structures are instrumental to the satisfaction of multifarious wants or private interests. With the risk of caricature, we might suppose that community is seen as a multitude moving diversely on a complex pattern of roadways. Some rules of the road are needed, and there is a common interest in making and servicing vehicles that hasten travel. But the pattern is itself indifferent to where any given individual is going, and the system of movements is a good one if it expedites the intent of each to approach her or his preferred destination.

By contrast, what I now wish to call the conservative ideal for community is not focused on satisfying private interests but, rather, on cultivating and exhibiting private virtue.[2] This ideal became especially visible in our broader public life during the closing decades of the twentieth century. Conservatives were a prominent part of the Reagan coalition and have since altered in their direction the shape of political discussion and public policy in the United States. I mean by "private virtue" moral traits or habits whose enactment does not require concern for the larger social or institutional order. Virtuous activities of this kind accept as given whatever shape the larger social structure may have, and a community can, within very generous limits, be inhabited by individuals of private virtue while remaining indifferent to alternative social arrangements. Being worthy of trust is, for instance, a trait all individuals can exhibit without concern for whether their society is equalitarian or aristocratic. As conservatives typically conceive them, private virtues give a person strength of character because they discipline wanton appetites for pleasure – and these habits typically include family commitment and sexual control, being responsible for oneself, readiness to work with

2. My discussion of American conservatives is indebted to Theodore J. Lowi, although he may not agree with all of my formulations (see Lowi).

diligence, obedience to the law and loyalty to local mores, charity toward the victim of misfortune, and religious piety.

This is one way to understand recent voices calling for "traditional values." As the term may suggest, conservatives can be tempted to define these values in narrow ways that rigidify parochial codes of an earlier time. For this reason, approved life forms are sometimes articulated in ways that are racist or sexist or that stigmatize legitimate diversity. Even worse, lip service to traditional morality can be merely a coded endorsement of racial and sexual prejudice. Still, the conservative view, as I mean to portray it, is not by definition discriminatory or resistant to change. What marks the ideal in its essence is this: Community is a bond that both sustains and is sustained by individuals of private virtue. Associational patterns should be controlled by a twofold point: on the one hand, to encourage, secure by social sanction, and, if necessary, enforce through law, the cultivation of such moral traits and, on the other, to provide the occasion for their expression. Accordingly, one's station in life, one's role in the communal structures of authority, power, privilege, or benefits and burdens, is not fundamentally important to human flourishing, because the purpose of our life together is to facilitate for each a life of good character.

Again with the risk of caricature, the metaphor useful for this ideal might be that of an army, organized into platoons having their own colors, arranged according to rank, and all marching in place.[3] Order within the whole depends on the discipline of each soldier as she or he occupies her or his station, and the discipline of each is sustained by the company of disciplined others and by the directions of those commissioned as leaders. The inclusive purpose of community is to establish and promote patterns of interaction in or through which lives of private virtue or responsibility are enhanced.

Having become prominent in national politics during the past few decades, this ideal might seem to be a recent addition to our public life. But contemporary conservatives inherit a considerable American tradition, which stretches back to Puritan colonies and includes the moral crusades of evangelical Christianity in the earlier nineteenth century. In our subsequent history, this commitment has been

---

3. The image of an army marking time is borrowed from its use to characterize Aristotle's account of nature (see Randall: 138).

persistently influential, but its long-standing presence is, by those who do not share it, easily overlooked. The industrial and later technological revolutions, including the dramatic advances in transportation and communication, have made the institutional structures of national life increasingly complex and significant, and focus naturally falls on these and thus on the dynamics of our federal government. In that context, as mentioned previously, the liberal ideal of community has, on the whole, been dominant.

Conservatives, by contrast, have typically focused on local communities as the proper context for cultivating private virtue and local governments as the effective facilitators, directing political attention to such matters as the public schools, the control of crime and vice, delinquency and other child-rearing problems, and the like. Prior to recent decades, union for national appearance occurred only on exceptional occasions, as in the temperance movement of the early twentieth century. We need not pause to explain the more sustained appearance since the 1970s, except to note that it principally seeks to roll back what are taken to be corrupting federal restrictions, in part through decisions of the Supreme Court, on the freedom of local communities and their governments to define and regulate the proper kind of local moral consensus (see Lowi: chap. 5). This is why the recent conservative movement sometimes seems to echo the call of an earlier era for "states' rights."

On my reading, a vast range of recent and current political contention in the United States, at least with respect to domestic issues, can be largely interpreted in terms of disagreements based on the liberal and conservative ideals I have summarily described, allowing that the former includes the quarrel between libertarian and welfare kinds of liberalism. In any event, cultivating and enacting private virtue is very different from satisfying private interests, and conservatives have often indicted the liberal sanction of want-satisfaction for permitting the base, undisciplined appetites inimical to a life of good character. Correspondingly, then, the liberal and conservative ideals define very different purposes for community. For all that, however, these two also have something they share. Both are evaluatively individualistic; each in its own way asserts or implies that the good life, the happy or flourishing life, is private, meaning that it is separated from the character or quality of our life in common.

On the liberal view, this follows because happiness is measured by interests or wants each person defines for herself or himself. To be sure, community is important for liberals because together we provide or promote resources instrumental to diverse satisfactions; in the nature of the case, however, a person's interests or wants in the relevant sense are finally a matter of her or his individual preference. On the conservative view, flourishing means a life of private moral character. To be sure, community is important for conservatives as the setting through which private virtue is developed and in which it is exhibited; finally, however, only one's own moral integrity matters. In one form or another, individualism in this sense may be the most pervasive communal ideal in American history, perhaps encouraged by early experience of a new world freed from the feudal legacies of Europe and, given disregard for the entitlements of Native Americans, magnified by open spaces where individuals or families could make it largely on their own. But whatever the historical sources, contemporary liberals and conservatives, their differences notwithstanding, join in perpetuating a view of the good life as separate from its associational participation. Insofar, then, they also conspire in setting a religious boundary that circumscribes the possibilities for public purpose.

III POLITICS AS A RELIGIOUS QUESTION

This religious boundary excludes justice as general emancipation. The individualism shared by these two ideals is contrary to Christian belief, which asserts a community of love as the principal worldly source and inclusive worldly end of the good life. On this belief, human flourishing is inseparable from our life together, because the chance for higher reaches of creative achievement is given by association with the achievements of others, and we make the most of the possibilities received when we direct them toward maximizing human mutuality. Because happiness is indefinable without reference to one's communities, a human individual may be called an individual-in-community. Moreover, the requisite communal bonds are not solely intimate or personal or local but, rather, stretch from these to the larger social and political orders, and the community of

love prescribes a politics that maximizes the extent of general emancipatory conditions to which all have equal access.

Marking this difference does not mean that Christians have no common ground with liberals or conservatives. Clearly, humans generally
do not flourish when they suffer economic want. As mentioned previously, the sources of empowerment include at their base the provision
for biological and material need and the expansion of those material
supports on which virtually all creative activity depends. The liberal
ideal, in its own way, appreciates this abiding fact. But Christian commitment parts company with liberals because their aim at maximal
want-satisfaction, constrained by national defense and certain equal
rights, at least permits the primacy of economic growth in the public
purpose and, therefore, the overriding importance of economic institutions in the social order. In contrast, the community of love calls
for economic provision only in the measure needed for maximal human mutuality, and thus associations aimed at instrumental goods
and services should be subservient to human association for its own
sake. Allowing that precise statement would be more nuanced, we
can still summarize the Christian difference in this way: Liberals reverse the proper order of value, designing our life together for other
ends, when, in truth, the latter are meant to serve the former.

Pursuit of the Christian ideal also coincides in part with a conservative focus on moral virtue. Mutuality is impossible or will quickly
become a mere shadow of itself if individuals take from their communities but do not contribute to them. Moreover, the requisite moral
character includes something like the so-called traditional values. Approach to the community of love is gravely threatened when dedication to intimate associations, personal responsibility, and charity for
those who suffer are widely missing. But Christian commitment parts
company with conservatives when they hold that private virtues are
sufficient to the good life. Thereby, the achievement in or through
which human life flourishes is reduced to moral character alone, and
the need for conditions of creativity provided or promoted by both
local and wider human communities is denied. If we speak in terms
of virtues, politics aimed at maximal mutuality adds the cultivation
of public virtue, which finally means nothing other than orientation
toward justice as general emancipation.

I will here simply assert my judgment that our contemporary political order falls far short of justice. On my accounting, the failure

extends to virtually all general conditions of empowerment, including economic provision, health care, education, associations of social support, vocational possibilities, respect for ethnic or cultural differences, treatment by the judicial system, and participation in the political process. In all of these cases, moreover, injustice is sometimes made the more severe by persisting structures of racial and sexual debasement. Our political faults, I further judge, derive in substantial part from widespread adherence to liberal and conservative ideals, and the next chapter will seek to illustrate this belief. Insofar as it is credible, Christians are led to conclude that their ideal for community is sorely overpowered in our public life, and politics as a common Christian vocation becomes the more urgent. But whether or not this is so, the burden here has been to illustrate how religious decisions can be at stake in the democratic political process. This intent will be aided by a further word about the understandings of ultimate worth connected with liberal and conservative ideals of community.

Pursued to its conclusion, the liberal ideal typically belongs to a secularistic or solely this-worldly answer to the religious question. To see human community as instrumental to want-satisfaction is to imply that human life finds its only significance in realizing whatever ends it sets for itself. Accordingly, liberals cannot consistently affirm that we exist for a purpose given in the nature of things or defined by a transcendent reality. Depending on how it is filled out, the conservative ideal may also be secularistic, tied to no ground of worth beyond the human adventure. When this is so, I expect, community as a bond among people of private virtue is a view typically found among the privileged classes, who associate their advantage with the well-being of the social order. At least unwittingly, then, the ideal serves to prevent discontent among the majority, who are counseled that they have all they need when they occupy their station with strength of character. But conservative views also appear with a populist appeal and, in that case, are typically theistic. To march virtuously in place, without concern for the larger social order, is seen to be sufficient because attention is focused on the individual's relation to God, so understood that the good life is independent of emancipation, and thus salvation can be disengaged from the pursuit of justice.

Perhaps an early expression of this separation occurred in the founding generation of the Massachusetts Bay Colony, established in 1630. At least if Perry Miller's reading is correct, the Puritans came to the New World on a mission, namely, to establish, in the words of John Winthrop, the "due forme of Government both civill and ecclesiasticall" as a "Citty upon a Hill" or a light to the world. New England was to be exemplary for England and for Europe more generally, where forms of the Reformation had failed to reach full accord with biblical ordinances and would be drawn to completion when provided with a model of perfection. This meant an undistracted working out of salvation within a church organized according to the congregational polity Puritan leaders took to be mandated by the New Testament, and within a civil order whose dominating purpose was to preserve that polity and thus to be "deliberately, vigorously, consistently intolerant" (Miller: 5). As a consequence, the "scheme of fixed and unalterable class distinctions" was affirmed as God's appointment and "this migration was specifically dedicated to an avowed end that had nothing to do with incomes" (Miller: 7, 8).

But whatever should finally be said about early Puritan purposes or those of other early American settlements, the subsequent Christian community in the United States often gave and still gives today aid and comfort to the conservative ideal. Between the Revolution and the Civil War, the more prevalent expression of Christian faith focused on the private virtues. Since it dominated religious life during this period, Protestant Christianity was, in its own way, a major force sustaining the pervasive individualism of earlier American life, which was also subsequently supported when some forms of Christian witness sanctioned the more or less unbridled pursuit of economic wealth after the Civil War. The social gospel, emerging with the new century in response to increasing complexity in American institutional life, was in significant measure an attempt to criticize and transform the complicity of the Christian churches with individualistic ideals.

Adherence in or through the social gospel to a differing ideal for community has been continued in various ways by certain Christians ever since, especially perhaps during the New Deal period and the 1960s, although this witness has, it is doubtless fair to say, voiced a minority opinion in American Christianity. In any event, the forceful appearance of conservatives in national politics during the final decades of the twentieth century embraced major participation by members of the Christian churches, especially through effective organizations summarily designated as representing the "Christian Right." At least in this sense, it is apt to speak of this participation as emerging from conservative Christian churches.

Christian complicity with the conservative ideal is, on my reading, the most apparent confirmation that the early account of political responsibility continues to be influential. If that account focused the moral task of Christians on the character and extension of the Christian community, in which the new life of Christian faith found social expression, the corresponding approval given to political quiescence was, as Augustine said, canceled when the governing authorities presented a hindrance to the church and its practice of true religion. On the Christian Right, summarily interpreted, the integrity and extension of the Christian community remain the principal context of moral concern, and the civil order is conceived as background for the distinct purpose of the church. The visible political activities might seem to pursue an ideal for the larger community But they are better seen as efforts to correct or prevent a larger social and political context taken to be decadent and thus a hindrance to formation within the church of private virtues taken to characterize the life of Christian faith. If, for Augustine, it does not matter "under whose rule a man lives, being so soon to die, provided that the rulers do not force him to impious or wicked acts" (1984: 205), this is because "the Heavenly City" is only on pilgrimage in this world, and "life will only be truly happy when it is eternal" (1984: 877, 590). In some formulation or other, I expect, this understanding of Christian faith continues to authorize those who maintain continuity with the early account. The abiding meaning of Christian faith separates the "felicity for which we should long" from the conditions of life "in this earthly city" (1984: 1067, 877). Hence, relation to God may be so understood that the good life does not depend on maximizing the access to general conditions of creativity equally available to all.

The present work is not the proper place for extended analysis of Augustine's theological legacy and, especially, its understanding of eternal life. It must suffice here to repeat that Augustine was among those who took for granted the basic presuppositions of Greek metaphysics and thus the conception of God as eternally complete. Whatever else such Christian thinkers may affirm about God's relation to the world or the world's relation to God, it remains that this idea of God asserts a gulf between time and eternity and, thereby, easily supports the view that true felicity occurs in another world and can be separated from the conditions of temporal life. So far as I can see, such an account of eternal life, like the idea of God to which it is connected, is finally inconsistent with the abiding Christian belief that our worth is ultimately grounded in the all-embracing love of God, which entails that unreserved love for God is expressed in love for all the world and thus pursuit of the community of love. In this respect, the theological understanding with which some Christians maintain continuity with the early account of political responsibility and thus support a conservative ideal of community must be called a misrepresentation of Christian faith.

But the so-called Christian Right does not exhaust contemporary Christians who disengage faith from justice as general emancipation. At least equally consequential is the focus in many so-called mainline churches on personal joy and suffering, intimate relationships, family life, the quality of local communities, and deeds or associations of charity. The validity of Christian witness in these respects, like the importance of private virtue, is not here at issue. What conflicts with the community of love is the widespread tendency to exclude political activity from common Christian witness. Within the churches I now have in mind, the effective grounds for this exclusion are not so thoroughly theological as when Christian belief is misrepresented in ways aligned with the conservative ideal for community. In these churches, rather, there is simply a withdrawal from political witness, leaving the political convictions of each Christian to some other mode of determination. Often, I expect, such indifference expresses the kind of complicity with given social and political conditions that betrays a dominating presence of individuals who are more economically and socially advantaged.

These judgments on contemporary American Protestantism need qualification. A full review of the religious situation would require proper recognition of Christians within so-called conservative churches who have sought to transform their political purposes in directions consistent with the community of love, and of Christians elsewhere, especially perhaps in African American churches, who have, sometimes to significant effect, advocated the political implications of Christian faith. But even after a more discriminate statement,

I believe, it will remain that Christian commitment to justice as general empowerment is not only substantially ineffective in public life but also a relatively weak voice in American Christianity. If this is so, then greater clarity about politics as a common Christian vocation is urgent, not only for our political community but also for the fidelity of contemporary Christian witness.

Chapter 6

Political Deliberations

God calls all to the community of love and thus to justice as general emancipation. Assuming that this assertion is both appropriately Christian and credible, this chapter seeks to illustrate its importance for specific political issues. I have chosen three current issues in American public life: abortion, affirmative action, and economic distribution. Together, they allow us to review the twofold character of justice in the community of love. The discussion of abortion is focused on the relevance of a democratic constitution and thus the formative rights of "we the people." Attention to the affirmative action debate exemplifies why the distinction between constitutional and substantive principles of justice is important. The assessment of economic distribution reasserts especially the substantive imperative to maximize the general conditions of creativity to which all have equal access.

In each case, as will be apparent, I have particular opinions about specific political directions Christian commitment commends. But these opinions also depend, increasingly so as we proceed through the three issues, on judgments regarding particular circumstances. Insofar, then, my conclusions cannot be derived solely from the principles of justice implied by Christian belief. Those who agree religiously might contest my readings of the relevant circumstances and, thereby, reach divergent political opinions. These discussions, moreover, do not adequately defend the more particular judgments involved. Hence, it may be useful to stress that the principal aim of this chapter is not to argue for specific political prescriptions. Although I do wish to speak for the conclusions, my main intent is to illustrate how Christian witness can make a difference in specific contemporary disagreements.

I ABORTION

If asked to point out public debates affected by religious convictions, contemporary Americans would, I expect, name two issues most often: on the one hand, our persisting difference over the propriety of religious expression in the public schools and, on the other, our persisting disagreement over whether and, if so, when abortion is permitted. Both of these issues became especially prominent following decisions by the United States Supreme Court. In 1962, the Court ruled that school prayer violates the constitutional prohibition on religious establishment, and in 1973, the decision in *Roe v. Wade* affirmed the right of pregnant women to have an abortion. To be sure, both issues evoked political contention prior to these decisions, especially within the local politics of the several states. In each case, however, the Court's ruling heightened the issue's national visibility and intensified its significance in electoral politics. In each case, therefore, national political life has been subsequently marked by vigorous opposition to the decision, including attempts to reverse it through constitutional amendment.

Of the two, the abortion debate has been the more fractious and, indeed, has occasioned violence. Many consider this question religious in some inherent way, because it seems so closely tied to fundamental questions about the nature and worth of human life. As is well known, the Christian churches themselves and, more generally, traditional religious communities have been deeply divided by the issue. Still, those divisions are simply part of a major conflict that finds most Americans, whether traditionally religious or not, aligned with one of the parties summarily characterized as "pro-life" or "pro-choice" – even if each party houses disagreement about the proper moral principle or the most circumspect political policy.

Given the brief treatment to which our present discussion must be confined, such profound differences preclude any hope of a definitive resolution, and this would be so even if abortion were not the especially vexing issue that, on my accounting, any sober view sees it to be. Still, I believe that something can be added through focus on the necessities of democracy as rule by way of full and free discourse. As Christians consider this issue, they will serve themselves and their political community by insisting that government by the people and thus equal constitutional rights are the political form of mutuality essential to the common good.

This approach takes for granted that morality and politics are not identical. The state is not authorized to determine in detail what morality requires and provide legal sanctions against all immoral action. To be sure, most who advocate governmental prohibition of all or virtually all abortions also believe this course to follow more or less directly from the immorality of the practice. They take abortion to be, save perhaps when the pregnant woman's life is at stake, an instance of murder, so that legal prohibition of abortion is implied by the state's responsibility to protect the right to life. As this reasoning suggests, however, moral conviction here leads to a political conclusion by virtue of another premise about the state's responsibilities, thereby confirming the difference, however close the connection, between the conviction and the conclusion. Moreover, no democratic citizen holds that all moral obligations should be legislated. For instance, promises ought to be kept, subject to specified exceptions; but no one holds that the state should define the exceptions and otherwise coercively enforce all promises in the manner of legal contracts.

In light of how divisive differences about abortion have become since *Roe v. Wade,* some say that the Court rendered a considerable disservice by deciding that the issue involves constitutional rights. On this view, the profound disagreements would have been more wisely given their due by leaving public determination in this instance to the statutory process within each of the states, where the relevant debates could yield nuanced decisions supported by local consensus or majority opinion. But this counsel assumes that no constitutional questions are implicated in the conflict over abortion. In fact, that assumption is wrong because the case for prohibition is correct at least in this: If abortion violates the state's prohibition of murder, the state has a constitutional duty to prohibit abortion. Given that a democratic constitution properly stipulates not only rights to certain public liberties, such as free speech and assembly, but also to certain private liberties, the right to life is surely the most basic, because all other rights depend on it.

With respect to this issue, then, the inherent constitutional question can be stated: Is a human fetus included within the population whose constitutional rights the state is bound to protect?[1] If the answer is affirmative, the state's policy with respect to abortion cannot be left to the statutory process. To the contrary, abortion can never be permitted, except perhaps to save the life of a pregnant woman, because the constitutional rights enjoyed by every member of "we the people" can never be transgressed by statutory law. On the assumption that constitutional provisions receive their authoritative interpretation from the Supreme Court, citizens committed to democratic justice have every reason to seek from the Court an answer to this question.

In *Roe v. Wade*, the Court ruled, at least implicitly, that an emerging human prior to birth is not a person *in the constitutional sense*, that is, in the sense that grounds a claim to constitutional rights. This ruling did not intend explicitly to say whether a fetus is a human being. The latter is the question many citizens take to be religious, so that, supposing the ruling to answer it, they also take the Court to violate the constitution's prohibition on religious establishment. But the Court meant to address what it deemed to be a distinct question: Is a human fetus included within the community of rights defined by the constitution? Whether that question is indeed distinct is, to be sure, contested, and we will pursue that issue in a moment. In any event, the Court's negative answer to its question is implied by its decision that abortion is, at least prior to viability, constitutionally permissible. As a constitutional person, a fetus would have a right to life that the state would be constitutionally bound to protect.

But the Court also said more. Not only is abortion constitutionally allowed but also its prohibition, at least during the first two trimesters, is constitutionally disallowed. Simply to rule that a fetus has no constitutional right to life means that statutory law is not unconstitutional when it permits abortion, leaving the possibility that legislatures would also act constitutionally were they to outlaw the practice. In contrast, *Roe v. Wade* further decided that pregnant women have a right to abortion that statutory law may not override, and one might question whether the Court had convincing grounds for this further determination. I will not examine the reasons offered by the Court. However those should be understood and assessed,

---

1. I am indebted in this discussion to Ronald Dworkin, although he may not agree with all of my conclusions (see Dworkin 1996: chaps. 1–4).

Christians and all citizens who affirm a democratic constitution can, I believe, readily see the logic of this further determination, once the constitutional status of the fetus is defined as the Court did.

Clarity might be aided by saying that what follows does not offer an interpretation in United States constitutional law. My use of "a democratic constitution" intends the kind of political framework for which this work previously argued, namely, one that stipulates formative principles for government by the people. In respects relevant to the issue of abortion, I think, the correspondence between a democratic constitution and the United States Constitution is sufficiently close that the distinction is inconsequential, but I will not defend that judgment. My concern is with abortion as a political issue within the kind of political community Christian faith prescribes. If or insofar as the United States Constitution or Supreme Court interpretations of it are inconsistent with democracy in this sense, Christians are also called to question that constitution or those interpretations.

To set forth the logic of a constitutional right to abortion, we need to restate that the right to life is only one, even if the most basic, of the rights to private liberties stipulated in a properly democratic constitution. Equal standing as a member of "we the people" also depends on the rights to control of one's own body and to freedom of conscience. Clearly, a statutory prohibition of abortion would restrict the liberty of a pregnant woman to control her own body in accord with her own conscience. To be sure, this freedom is not absolute and, like all constitutional liberties, may be restricted in order to protect the rights of all others to those very liberties. For this reason, to cite one instance, prohibitions on taking certain addictive drugs are, I believe, constitutional, given that their use often occasions behavior abusive to the rightful freedom of others, and it is not feasible to enforce laws that discriminate among various users. But the imperative condition of such restrictions is this: They must apply to all members of the community, so that equal rights to control of one's own body are honored. In contrast, a proscription of abortion would violate a pregnant woman's equal constitutional rights because men who participate in the reproductive process would encounter no remotely similar restrictions on their liberty. The right to bodily control would have acutely different meanings for men and women, and the inequality would be the more severe because a woman's decision about abortion involves fundamental matters of conscience.

134

If a human fetus is excluded from the constitutional community, in other words, abortion cannot be prohibited by statute because doing so violates the formative equality of "we the people" and thus the political mutuality prescribed by God's call to a community of love. But this conclusion depends on the prior determination that a human fetus is not a person in the constitutional sense, and many citizens, including many Christians, find compelling grounds to oppose the Court's decision in this respect. A human fetus, they believe, is not merely a potential but, rather, an actual human being, who cannot be distinguished in any relevant sense from a person subsequent to birth. Hence, an emerging human prior to birth has a constitutional right to life. If a legal ban on abortion conflicts with a woman's equal right to bodily control, these citizens resolve that her right must here be forfeited. Equality between men and women cannot here be protected because the unborn's right to life takes precedence over the constitutional rights of a pregnant woman, unless her own life is at stake. On this view, the Court did indeed read into the constitution a dogmatic statement about the nature of humanity. If such statements are religious in character, then the Court in fact announced that the constitution explicitly takes sides in a religious disagreement.

But the Court's ruling, I believe, can be defended without explicitly deciding whether a fetus is a human being. The relevant backing is, instead, the nature of democracy as politics by the way of reason, which means that no claim for ultimate terms of political assessment and, therefore, no other claim should determine governmental activities unless it can be redeemed by public argument. Since constitutional principles themselves determine activities of the state, no provision should be constitutionally stipulated unless it, too, can be validated through full and free discourse. Indeed, democratic citizens have special cause to insist on this standard when their constitution is at issue, precisely because it stipulates the conditions for the argumentative practice through which all common decisions are properly taken. In refusing constitutional rights to a fetus, then, we are not bound explicitly to deny that human life begins before birth. We need only find that this belief cannot be validated by the kind of argument required to determine the scope of the constitutional community.

For our discussion here I will assume this finding; that is, no such argument for this belief can be given, and reasons for it will always depend on a premise or prior conviction that cannot itself be debated but must be merely accepted. Naturally, my assumption may be rejected, and I readily concede that, were it challenged by a public argument, the conclusions I will reach could not be sustained without showing that argument to fail. Still, the absence of convincing public reasons for the human being of a fetus is, so far as I can see, widely acknowledged, even by most who disagree with the Court's ruling. In contrast, our humanity on being born, I will also assume, is not only noncontroversial but also can be redeemed in public discourse. Naturally, this second assumption may also be contested, and I also readily concede that my discussion here cannot be successful unless the assumption is valid. The discussion here, then, seeks to show the consequences of these two assumsptions.

I recognize that some will object to combining the two assumptions. On their view, any convincing argument for the humanity of a newborn child will also establish the humanity of a fetus. There can be no relevant difference between them because both have merely a potential to develop the features by which humans are typically distinguished from nonhuman creatures – for instance, self-consciousness, the use of reason, the use of language, and the like. Hence, any convincing argument that fails to include a fetus within the human community must also fail to include newborn children, and if abortion is permissible, then so, too, is infanticide. But there is this difference between a fetus and a newborn child: Legal protection for the potential of a fetus conflicts with the equal right of a pregnant woman to control her own body; legal protection for the potential of a newborn child does not. So far as I can see, then, a convincing argument for our humanity on being born need not be an argument for the humanity of a fetus because what is thereby established may be something like the following understanding: All creatures who are self-conscious or potentially self-conscious and can be included in accord with their stage of development in a community of equal rights to private and public liberties (including, therefore, rights to life and to control of one's own body) are human beings. On this understanding, a fetus and a newborn child are distinct because the criterion stipulates two conditions – not only actual or potential self-consciousness but also inclusion within a community of *equal* rights to private and public liberties. A newborn child can, and a fetus cannot, be so included because granting a fetus a right to life denies that women and men have an equal right to control of their own bodies.

To be sure, one might question whether both conditions are necessary to being human. But this question would be relevant only if the proposed understanding is taken to be a definition of all human beings. To the contrary, the point is to establish something sufficient to being human, and thus the understanding purports to define at least some human beings. Whatever other creatures may or may not be members of the human community, in other words, creatures of the kind described belong to it; whatever the adequate definition of all humans may be, it must affirm our humanity on being born. In this sense, that affirmation may be defended by convincing argument even while the wider question of whether a fetus is a human being is not addressed. Still, I will not here seek to provide the argument for our humanity on being born.[2] My discussion is limited to showing the consequences of the two assumptions – that the human being of a fetus cannot, and our humanity on being born can, be established by public argument.

I further recognize that testing the two assumptions requires exploration of what counts as convincing public argument for one or another understanding of creatures as human beings. This, too, is a contested matter, just as, more generally, politics by the way of reason must somehow come to terms with conflicting accounts of reason. In the present context, however, the essential point is this: Convincing public argument excludes any validation dependent on one or more premises that cannot be, when contested, themselves redeemed by

2. The argument I have in mind seeks to show that every claim to moral validity presupposes a meta-ethical principle of equal respect for all actual and potential communication partners – where equal communicative respect can be explicated in terms of the rights to private and public liberties – and, further, that this principle is itself finally validated by the inclusive moral purpose discussed earlier in this text, namely, to maximize in the long run mutuality among individuals who live with self-understanding. I have sought to clarify and defend this meta-ethical principle in Gamwell 2000 (see especially chap. 4). Let us grant that this or some other argument will establish the humanity of individuals who can be included, according to their stage of development, within a community of equal rights to private and public liberties. It then follows that one argument for the humanity of a fetus – summarized, apparently with approval, by Michael Perry – is unsuccessful. "Because there is no nonarbitrary way to draw the bounds of the human community at any point short of conception, we must treat a human fetus as a member of the human community" (Perry: 71). In fact, the antecedent in this argument asserts what the argument intends to show, specifically, that birth is an arbitrary boundary for the human community. If we can redeem in public discourse our humanity on being included within a community of equal communicative rights, drawing the bounds at birth is arbitrary only if the humanity of a fetus can also be so redeemed. Hence, the argument summarized by Perry depends on there being some other convincing argument for including a fetus in the human community.

argument. Thus, ultimate terms of political assessment cannot themselves be established by appeal to their authoritative presentation
in some specific religious community or tradition or cultural inheritance. Although views of good argument may themselves conflict,
the way of reason entails that these differences, too, are subject to discourse and cannot be adjudicated by authority. Full and free discourse
means that convincing reasons are finally authorized by common human experience, that is, by what is present to all who might join in
the argument, however different their lives may be in detail.[3] In this
sense, then, I assume that the humanity of a fetus cannot, and our
humanity on being born can, be redeemed by public reasons.

Some may now object that excluding a fetus from the human community also lacks convincing public argument. This objection is, I
believe, mistaken. More extended reflection, I am inclined to think,
would conclude that a fetus is not a human being in the relevant
moral sense. But this conclusion purports to answer the immensely
controversial question of an adequate definition of humanity and thus
could not receive convincing defense without the kind of expanded
treatment only another work could offer. For present purposes, then,
the objection is mistaken because irrelevant. Whether or not denying
the actual humanity of a fetus also lacks convincing public argument
makes no difference to the constitutional question. This is because
"person" in the constitutional sense must have a definition; without
it, there can be no determination of who is a member of "we the
people" and hence of the democratic community of rights. Since the
people govern themselves through full and free discourse, the constitutional definition must be limited to what can be validated by public
argument. In other words, inclusion bears the burden of redemption.
By this criterion, and given our assumptions, the boundary belongs
at birth. The point may be restated in terms of the following three
beliefs: (1) a human fetus is distinctively human; (2) a human fetus
is not distinctively human; (3) an individual on being born of human

3. Whatever else it does or does not involve, then, convincing public argument requires
the following: The conclusions it advocates articulate or specify principles that cannot be consistently denied, because affirmation of them is implied by every possible
assertion or denial. So far as I can see, there is no other way to avoid a premise that
is merely asserted. In its concluding section, Chapter 4 suggested how Christians
might redeem their belief about the ultimate ground of worth through reasons authorized by common human experience. For further discussion of argument that
validates and invalidates religious convictions, see the Appendix.

parents is distinctively human. If the third alone can be established by convincing public reasons, it properly determines the subjects of constitutional rights. Accordingly, the first belief cannot define a constitutional person, and this is so even if the second belief is also beyond argumentative redemption.

This account may raise another objection: Allowing that both the first and second beliefs may be beyond convincing public argument undermines the way of reason itself, since, in that case, it cannot validate and invalidate answers to the question: Is a fetus a distinctively human being? That objection is, I think, also mistaken. Commitment to full and free discourse affirms that reasons authorized by common human experience are sufficient to validate any understanding that can be validated, and it does not follow that all true understandings can be validated. Perhaps, for instance, true answers to some questions about our own primal self-understanding and thus our deepest motives in acting as we do cannot be established by argument. In this sense, certain questions may be nondiscursive. When faced with a question of this kind, critical reflection has no alternative except to suspend judgment, and if action requires a resolution, one can only decide on whatever personal grounds one finds compelling.

But, then, answers to such questions cannot properly claim the status pertinent to democratic decision making. What finally defines politics by way of full and free discourse is its affirmation that the religious question *is* discursive, meaning that claims for ultimate terms of political assessment can be argumentatively assessed. Were this not the case, argument by appeal to common human experience could not finally validate any political claims at all. And because the question of ultimate terms is discursive, no political assessment properly determines the state's activities unless it can be established by public argument.[4] If no claim for the humanity of a fetus can be redeemed

---

4. Some theories of democracy criticized in Chapter 2 hold, as we may now say, that the religious question is nondiscursive and, given this assumption, propose to separate principles of justice from any "comprehensive doctrine" or conception of the comprehensive good. So far as I can see, no such understanding of the religious question could itself be redeemed by argument, and this is why those theories are inconsistent with popular sovereignty. If some questions are nondiscursive, then, commitment to the way of reason implies that discourse is able nonetheless to establish which questions are of this kind. For instance, if a question about our own primal self-understanding has a valid answer discourse cannot validate, the fact that this question is of this kind must itself be open to argumentative redemption,

in this way, the democratic commitment to validation through discourse is sufficient to command our agreement with the Court's determination.

On this accounting, moreover, attempts so to amend the constitution as to include a fetus within the community of rights are inconsistent with the democratic community they affirm, because they seek a constitutional stipulation that cannot be redeemed in full and free discourse. If we accept both of the preceding assumptions (that the humanity of a fetus cannot, and our humanity of being born can, be established by public argument), then the constitutional liberties of a pregnant woman cannot be restricted by the presumed rights of the fetus she carries. The coerced limitation a statutory prohibition of abortion would place on her control of her own participation in the reproductive process is unconstitutional. As having rights to private liberties, she must have a thorough opportunity to consider the possibility of abortion, seeking whatever counsel she deems important, and the right to effect the decision she takes. The Court has determined that this liberty is protected if, dangers to the woman's health aside, she can terminate her pregnancy during the period prior to viability. Whether this was a good decision can also be debated. But the issue in that debate is circumscribed by consensus on the basic constitutional point.

If Christians can join this consensus because democracy is required by the community of love, God also calls all people to a reverence for all life, a summons of which pregnant women generally are acutely aware. Moreover, the duty of a democratic state to protect the rights of all gives it reason to be concerned when something threatens widely to erode respect for the inherent worth of human life. Citizens who share such respect may yet disagree on its meaning for personal decisions about abortion. But it is not unreasonable to think that opinions in which those decisions are trivialized would, if pervasive, be such a threat. Thus, the state is not barred from promoting a general attitude

perhaps through analyzing the fragmentary character of our self-consciousness. If the question of whether a fetus is distinctively human is also of this kind, one does not imply an answer in deciding that a positive answer cannot be redeemed by argument. As mentioned, I am inclined to think that this question is *not* nondiscursive. On that view, the Court's decision *implies* a denial of humanity to a fetus. Even then, however, the constitutional ruling does not explicitly decide to this effect; to the contrary, the only stipulation is that inclusion of a fetus within the constitutional community cannot be redeemed by argument.

in which decisions about an emerging human prior to birth are taken with the seriousness they merit. To make this point is not to say that only the decision to abort can be made superficially. In light of some moral and religious commitments, the decision to conceive or, having conceived, to give birth may, in certain circumstances, be against the counsel of serious consideration. Still, those who agree that a pregnant woman's basic liberties include her right to choose should not blindly assume that all political attempts to set conditions in which abortions may occur are designed to undermine *Roe v. Wade*. Prescribing a day of wait for reconsideration, for instance, could have another and legitimate public purpose. All the consequences of such a law must be examined, but it is not transparently unconstitutional.

In addition, the state is not barred from considering the interests of life that does not have constitutional rights. Legislation may define humane treatment of animals, for instance, especially when they have the capacity to suffer, and the democratic process may well find a special state responsibility when the life in question is an emerging human being. If political equality is generally secured by protecting a woman's freedom during the first two trimesters, then the state may be permitted to prohibit abortions, absent danger to the life or health of the woman, in the later stage of pregnancy. Perhaps the people can decide that, having carried the pregnancy thus far, she has chosen for the emerging human being, just as the man who shared in conception has legally committed himself to care and support for the child, should she decide to give birth. Even this permission, however, would be limited by the possibility of special circumstances in which the woman in question could not earlier exercise her right, and there is room to doubt whether such a law could be so drafted as to provide effectively for these exceptions. In other words, the state's purposes, here as always, are never allowed to violate or burden any individual's constitutional rights. If there are legitimate constraints on the occurrence of abortion, this can only mean that they do not harm each woman's right to consult her own conscience and to terminate her pregnancy if she so decides. Further, this right belongs to all pregnant women equally, so that state action may not impose burdens on those who suffer economic disadvantage.

This discussion, it is worth repeating, has focused solely on the question of abortion as it occurs in the context of a Christian's political vocation. The profound moral question faced by an individual woman remains. God's call to mutuality in all its forms summons religious communities to provide counsel to their members and urges us all to pursue greater moral insight and sensitivity in meeting our personal responsibilities as participants in the reproductive process. I will not seek to specify those responsibilities. The point here is, rather, that a democratic political community has its own requirements, the relevant one being that resolution of political questions turns on what can and cannot be established by the way of reason. If the assumptions I have made are valid, this necessary condition is in the present case sufficient for limits on the state's activities. Whatever persisting disagreements will be expressed in our continuing discussion of human reproduction, we may share a commitment to the democratic way as the political form of our common life and commonly affirm a pregnant woman's constitutional right to make her own decision about whether to give birth.

Christians for whom this conclusion specifies justice to this issue thereby have cause to contest the claims of those who disagree. In the context of this work, then, it is pertinent to ask whether one or more alternative religious views are implicated in current efforts to make abortion illegal. This is more or less obviously the case insofar as citizens pursue that end because they accept the official Roman Catholic position. But I will not attempt to summarize that position or its relation, debated among Roman Catholics, to the responsibilities of the state. Having in mind the previous chapter, I wish especially to observe how the conservative ideal of community is also expressed in the contemporary debate about this issue. Those persuaded, however inchoately, that community is primarily a bond among individuals of private virtue typically believe that abortion is inconsistent with sexual responsibilities central to the life of moral character. They also hold that government has the duty to help inculcate the relevant virtues.

In no way do I question that many conservatives firmly believe in the actual humanity of a fetus. Insofar as it backs their political opposition to abortion, however, this conviction is, I suspect, inseparable from an inclusive account of sexual responsibility that conservatives take to be profoundly threatened in a culture they find all too pervasively influenced by the liberal ideal of maximizing want-satisfaction and thus by sexual permissiveness. Accordingly, *Roe v.*

Wade is seen as a prototypical case of the control this liberal ideal exercises over decisions of the federal government. On the basis of this reading, we can estimate that widespread commitment to private virtue as sufficient to, or at least paramount in, the good life heightens the intensity with which *Roe v. Wade* is rejected and legal prohibition of abortion is pursued. But Christians have an ideal for community contrary to those of both liberals and conservatives. Having in view the community of love, Christians can affirm the equal rights of women essential to popular sovereignty without thereby sacrificing the importance of private virtue in general or sexual responsibility in particular, insisting only that these virtues are properly conceived in relation to the aim at maximal mutuality and thus justice as general emancipation. If something like the reading I have offered is correct, moreover, Christians have reason to say that a religious decision is at stake in our continuing debate about reproductive rights.

II AFFIRMATIVE ACTION

When the papers of former Supreme Court Justice William O. Douglas were opened a few years ago, they disclosed an uncertainty about affirmative action shared by many Americans. In 1971, Douglas held the court's swing vote in a case that posed the issue. Marco DeFunis had been denied admission to the University of Washington Law School, even though his grades and aptitude test scores were superior to those of most African American students who were accepted. He sued. The State Supreme Court of Washington upheld the university's action, and the United States Supreme Court agreed to hear Defunis's appeal. To all appearances, Douglas was, as Nicholas Lemann summarizes, "genuinely torn." A "fiery liberal and champion of the downtrodden who had come down on the side of blacks in every landmark civil rights case," Douglas also opposed racial preferences. After several drafts that argued the matter to differing conclusions, his final draft opposed reverse discrimination but let the Washington court's decision stand. He escaped the apparent contradiction by indicting the Law School Aptitude Test (LSAT) as racially biased, even though he had no evidence to support this claim. "So," Lemann concludes, "he went through every possible feeling one can have about affirmative action . . . and wound up throwing up his hands" (Lemann: 52).[5]

Since its inception in the 1960s, affirmative action has come to mean many things. Originally a description of special efforts to solicit minority applicants, it now includes the favoring of women and minorities over men and whites who, as judged by test scores or other prevailing criteria, are equally or better qualified. In part, the practice has developed voluntarily, but some of its better-known forms occur through governmental mandates. Although punctuated by controversy from time to time, the evolution of affirmative action proceeded with minimal dissent until the past ten or fifteen years, when major opposition to virtually all forms of the practice emerged.

Many critics charge that some affirmative action programs have allowed widespread abuse and that most have failed to serve their stated purpose, namely, to help correct the consequences of generations of institutional discrimination. But this indictment is typically coupled with a principled insistence that affirmative action, whatever its results, is inherently unjust or unfair, committing the very kind of injustice whose persisting effects it is supposed to correct. Against all forms of the practice, we are told, our public life should always be blind to differences of religion, race, gender, or ethnic origin. Any denial of this principle is an offense to human dignity, and to justify current violations as responses to violations in the past is a practical contradiction. However worthy the ends sought, reverse discrimination is no less discrimination.

We may recognize that attacks on affirmative action are sometimes covert attempts to maintain established patterns of racial and gender advantage. Still, the moral vision of a society fair to all is profoundly important to many citizens. Even some who protest that minorities and women are often denied equal access to the social conditions of human flourishing and consider redress an important public purpose nonetheless question affirmative action and thus share the

---

5. The United States Supreme Court never decided the case. DeFunis had, in fact, won his suit in a lower Washington court and "entered the law school under a court order." The Washington State Supreme Court reversed that decision in upholding the university's action. In agreeing to hear DeFunis's appeal, the United States Supreme Court stayed the decision of the Washington State Supreme Court, allowing Defunis to remain in the university's law school. The justices of the United States Supreme Court subsequently declared the case moot. "The stated reason was that DeFunis was about to graduate . . . and the underlying reason was that no clear majority position on the issue was emerging" (Lemann: 52).

uncertainty of Justice Douglas. In their commitment to the community of love, I believe, Christians have grounds to address this uncertainty and thus to aid in a significant way the democratic resolution of this issue. As I will try to show, the difference between constitutional and substantive principles of justice, implied by the ideal of maximal mutuality, is especially important to this contribution. I will take for granted that the problems affirmative action means to address are both real and acute, and I will further assume that some present or possible programs (relating to, for instance, employment decisions, governmental contract awards, or higher education admissions) do or could have important positive effects. Clarity will be advanced, I believe, by focus on the more fundamental resistance to affirmative action.

In the United States Constitution, the relevant provision is part of the Fourteenth Amendment, which prescribes "equal protection of the laws." As with the previous discussion of abortion, however, the argument here does not intend an interpretation in United States constitutional law.[6] My concern is affirmative action within a democratic political community constituted by formative principles of justice. This focus is, I judge, pertinent to our contemporary debate because the issue is, for many citizens, primarily a moral one. They wonder whether affirmative action violates a basic moral principle essential to democratic politics. On a proper interpretation of the Fourteenth Amendment, the words cited from it may well articulate the relevant formative principle I will discuss. But I use those words here only because a properly democratic constitution includes a guarantee for which "equal protection of the laws" is a thoroughly apt formulation.

Because government by the people entails the equality of all as always potential and sometimes actual participants in full and free political discourse, equal protection belongs among the constitutional rights to public and private liberties. It means that no law can prescribe differential treatment of individuals solely because they exhibit some natural or historically created difference, that is, a difference not created by relevant decisions the individuals have made. In a full and free discourse, the only differences that matter concern the validity of claims, the force of arguments, and the commitment of individuals

---

6. In that context, there may or may not be cause for Justice Douglas's uncertainty, although I suspect that his dilemma also expressed his own moral convictions.

to common pursuit of the truth. Hence, all natural and historically created differences are constitutionally irrelevant to the state's activities. For instance, no law can prescribe differential burdens or benefits solely on the basis of differences in race or gender or ethnicity. Doing so asserts that the difference has fundamental moral importance, as if it marks a difference in status among "we the people." The constitutional equality essential to popular sovereignty is denied, and this equality is what gives apparent validity to the view that affirmative action is inherently unjust.

But clarity about the principle also provides the context for assessing that view. If justice means the formative equality of all, does it follow that natural and historically created differences are never pertinent to substantive activities of the state, so that differential treatment on this basis is never permitted? Consider what that interpretation implies. It would be unconstitutional to exempt older people from military conscription or entitle them to special treatment, since differences in age are natural. Similarly, all statutes prescribing differential advantage on the basis of physical circumstance, for instance, special support for those who are physically challenged or mentally impaired or who are victims of natural disasters, would violate the constitution. Indeed, we would need to question any law that requires differential treatment based on differences in past performance or present abilities, since these differences are due in part to talents and opportunities that are naturally given or historically created. A law that prescribes admission to public law schools based on past grades and LSAT scores, or one that prescribes selection for governmental employment on the basis of civil service examinations, would be suspect. Although differences in ability may result in part from people's efforts to develop their potentialities, how could the relevant institutions ever decide whether or to what extent superior capacities derive from individual initiative rather that beneficial conditions?

In fact, we have many laws that discriminate on the basis of natural and historically created differences and that no one calls unconstitutional because the differential treatment serves some other end. Keeping formative and substantive justice distinct helps make sense of such statutes, because it follows that formative or constitutional equality is not equality with respect to all substantive political purposes. To the contrary, equal protection of the laws means that natural and historically created differences cannot *in themselves* justify differential treatment, as if those differences had some fundamental moral importance. But the entire point of a democratic constitution is the pursuit of substantive justice through popular rule. Hence, equality defined by the constitutional right in question can only mean that natural and historically created differences are irrelevant *unless* the people plausibly decide that differential treatment is, while otherwise constitutional, important to the common good. The law is then justified by a substantive purpose, for instance, raising an army, staffing the government effectively, or relieving the suffering of people who are victims of circumstances beyond their control.

In sum, democratic citizens should distinguish constitutional issues from issues of justice within the democratic process. To be sure, questions about the framework are also questions of justice, because the constitution stipulates formative principles of a just political process. But only some questions of justice are about constitutional requirements. The public school segregation declared inherently unjust by the United States Supreme Court in 1954 did indeed violate constitutional principles because the practice served no recognizable purpose except to assert that differences in race have in themselves moral importance. In contrast, a law prescribing that the applicant's academic record alone shall be relevant for admission to a public university – enacted, say, because the democratic process plausibly decides that this rule for selection serves the long-term welfare of the community – may or may not be unjust. But it is not unconstitutional, even if the differential treatment it prescribes is based on differences due in large part to naturally given talents and historically created opportunities.

In like manner, our debate about affirmative action cannot be settled by the constitutional right to equal protection of the laws. These programs do not assert the fundamental moral importance of differences in race or gender. To the contrary, affirmative action serves a substantive purpose: to help correct the consequences of generations of institutionalized discrimination. As we have noted, some argue that the practice is not effective in pursuit of its aim. But I have here assumed that some forms of affirmative action do or would contribute to their end in order to clarify that the relevant question of principle is not constitutional but, rather, concerns substantive justice. That question leaves considerable room for disagreement among those who differ about substantive political principles. But there is no cause for uncertainty occasioned by supposing that affirmative action violates the constitutional equality of "we the people."

If the practice can be effective, Christians have reason to support it. In the community of love, substantive justice maximizes the access to general emancipatory conditions that is equally available. Indifference or opposition to affirmative action could be consistent with that principle only if (a) generations of discrimination against women and minorities have not resulted in acute and persisting denial of their just access to conditions of creative achievement or (b) all things considered, effective forms of affirmative action somehow otherwise lessen the extent of generally emancipatory conditions that is equally available to all. The former is not credible, and I am not aware of any plausible argument for the latter.

Even if affirmative action advances the common good, some may object, it still seems, at least in some instances, unfair. But this perception repeats the confusion of formative and substantive principles of justice. So far as political purposes are concerned, "fairness" can only be defined by what is just, and the term itself, therefore, has two correspondingly distinct meanings. Constitutional fairness means equal standing as a member of "we the people" and is articulated in rights to public and private liberties. In contrast, fairness as a standard for activities of the state depends on the substantive character of justice. If politics is properly directed to the community of love, effective affirmative action is indeed fair, because maximizing the general empowerment equally available is the only substantive meaning fairness could have. To suppose that Christians must sacrifice fairness to the common good is, then, to betray the influence of some other principle of justice and, thereby, some other communal ideal.

Assuming this analysis to be essentially correct, Christians might also serve the political community by seeking the sources of basic moral opposition to affirmative action. Whatever else has informed recent attacks on the practice, I expect that both liberal and conservative ideals of community have been consequential. To be sure, many liberals have supported affirmative action. Liberalism, we mentioned, appears in two expressions, which commonly call for maximal satisfaction of private interests or wants and differ in the following way: For libertarian liberals, as I called them, the inclusive end prescribes minimizing governmental control and maximizing liberty as freedom from interference, thereby maximizing voluntary association, especially transactions through the free market. For welfare liberals, the state is duty-bound to promote the basic welfare of individuals; that is, justice requires that some basic level of certain prerequisites to pursuit of one's private interests be provided for all. Liberal politics representing this second expression has typically endorsed policies that seek to correct inherited consequences of discrimination and thus has advocated affirmative action in some form or other.

In contrast, libertarian politics has typically opposed the practice. Requiring the state to protect equal liberty, many libertarians readily denounce racial, sexual, and other forms of discrimination as inconsistent with the democratic ideal. In view of the same norm, however, affirmative action practiced by public institutions is more or less obviously a kind of coercive governmental activity inimical to a free society. Still, if libertarians have had an effect in recent public discussion, the issue has become prominent because conservatives have joined the opposition. Because they measure human flourishing by the cultivation and exercise of private virtue, including habits of honest and disciplined work, many conservatives also condemn racial and other forms of discrimination as a breach of treatment in accord with moral character. But affirmative action is seen to be similarly destructive of a good community. Individuals who, by traditional criteria, merit the award of contracts or positions are denied a response appropriate to their dispositions and dedication, and those who do not deserve favor are rewarded. Society fails, on the one side, to reinforce good character and, on the side of those improperly favored, to cultivate it.

On this reading, then, both libertarians and conservatives find that affirmative action more or less directly violates what they take to be basic moral principles for the social order. Although different, the principles in question commonly prescribe evaluative individualism. Both define the good life primarily in terms of something separate from our common life, either private interests or private moral character, and call for social structures designed accordingly. For differing reasons, then, both ideals militate against the general public purpose prescribed by Christian faith and, specifically, the conviction that human flourishing depends on its communities as the principal worldly source of empowerment. Both alternatives conflict with the assessment of affirmative action in view of our political responsibility to maximize the access to general conditions of creativity equally available to all.

In sum, political forces opposed to the practice are informed in part by substantive principles of justice at odds with justice as general emancipation. Moreover, the commitment of these contrary ideals to individualistic conceptions of the good life may also help explain why debate about affirmative action so often fails to distinguish substantive political principles from constitutional rights. Understood as basic principles of individualism, both the libertarian view of a free society and the conservative account of a moral community are easily taken to be constituting principles of American democracy and are thereby confused with the formative definition of "we the people." Accordingly, citizens who censure the nation's history of institutional discrimination may nonetheless mistakenly conclude that affirmative action violates the same constitutional principles by which that history is condemned. Be that as it may, the measure in which libertarian and conservative ideals regulate the responses of citizens to effective programs of affirmative action is the measure in which politics pursued as a Christian vocation should recognize religious differences at stake in the democratic discourse.

III ECONOMIC DISTRIBUTION

Calling economic distribution a political issue is, in one sense, misleading. Unlike abortion and affirmative action, the distribution of income and wealth has not itself occasioned conspicuous contention during recent decades. To be sure, the economic effects of policies and proposed policies on various segments or groups in American society are continually contested, and welfare and libertarian liberals debate whether or in what ways the state should provide or promote some basic level of economic support for all citizens. But our democratic discourse has been largely silent about whether justice permits the current extent of income and wealth inequality. In this sense, economic distribution has not been an issue. In another sense, however, an issue is present when there is injustice, and I will suggest that economic inequality calls for sustained public attention.

If abortion as a political question is primarily constitutional, and if our debate about affirmative action has confused formative principles and substantive goals, the character of this third issue seems more or less clearly to be substantive. Membership in "we the people," and thus constitutional rights to public and private liberties, do not explicitly define the economic distribution justice provides or promotes. For those who pursue the community of love, therefore, the relevant principle is justice as general emancipation: Maximize the general conditions of creativity to which all have equal access.

This principle, as we have noted, directs attention to many conditions of creativity. Other things being equal, people are more emancipated by greater access to physical and psychological well-being, including good habits; economic provision and opportunity; educational attainment and opportunity; a rich cultural context; beauty and integrity in the nonhuman world, both natural and artificial; and, implicated by all these as well as for its own sake, a favorable pattern of human association, including freedom of association. Thus, decisions in accord with justice as general emancipation require judgments about the relations among these several conditions. The principle cannot mean maximizing the measure in which each condition is equally available to all, since some of the conditions are, or in some circumstances may be, competitive; enhancing one is possible only by reducing or failing to enhance one or more others. For instance, economic provision may be lessened by protecting environmental beauty, the resources available to educate all members of the community may be decreased by an increased measure of health care, and the extent to which freedom of association is present may at some point be sacrificed by increasing the measure of most other general conditions equally available. Justice as general emancipation cannot be applied to the issue of economic distribution as if it were the only relevant condition of creativity, and we will have occasion later to revisit this point.

Still, economic provision is especially important to one's creative opportunities, both in itself and as a prerequisite for other kinds of access, and thus our contemporary distribution of income and wealth should be assessed in relation to the aim at general empowerment. This is the more urgent because economic inequality increased dramatically in the United States during the last quarter of the twentieth century. Beginning the new millennium, this country "has the most unequal income distribution and one of the highest poverty rates among all the advanced economies in the world" (Mishel, Bernstein, and Schmitt: 11). Whatever other forces were at work, moreover, they were abetted by the virtual absence of protest from either major political party. Throughout the period, political leadership in both parties saw no need for – or, at least, refrained from – any substantial challenge to wealth and income distributions themselves. Encompassing economic statistics and comparisons are, naturally, complicated matters, permitting legitimate disputes about how results are properly reached. To the best of my knowledge, however, the summary figures I will offer, always adjusted for inflation, are beyond significant dispute. If differing calculations would alter the outcome, the changes would be relatively slight, and the stark conclusions about economic inequality would only be confirmed. The focus here is on income distribution, but this understates the matter, because it is noncontroversial that wealth inequality is even greater (see Mishel et al. 2001: 260–1; Phillips: 79).[7]

Following World War II, the United States income distribution moved toward greater equality for some three decades. The share of income going to the lowest 20% or "quintile" of households[8] increased, while that going to the highest 20% and to the highest 5% both decreased (Mischel et al. 2001: 49–54; Phillips: 137). Summarily speaking, the distance between rich and poor narrowed to the smallest in the nation's history. Since the mid-1970s, the country has marched steadily in the other direction. The gap between the most and least advantaged has stretched back through and well beyond what it was prior to the postwar reduction. This march, quickened in the 1980s, slowed in the 1990s, especially during the economic boom and low unemployment of the century's final five years, but even then inequality continued to expand (Mischel, Bernstein, and Boushey: 51f.).

Using data from the Congressional Budget Office, one analysis shows that average income in the lowest quintile of households actually decreased between 1977 and 1999, while that in the highest quintile increased by more than 30% and that in the highest 5% by more than 50%. The results are the same both before and after taxes.

7. In 1998, the top fifth held more than 80% of all household wealth while receiving some 50% of household income (Mishel et al. 2001: 260).
8. "Households" as used in official statistics on income distribution does not mean the same as "families," because the former includes people living alone. But the difference this makes is indifferent to the general trends and orders of magnitude summarized in this discussion.

Indeed, average income for the lower 60% was summarily stagnant over these two decades, so that virtually all income enhancement went to the upper 40%. While incomes in the lower and middle quintiles grew during the 1990s, especially after 1995, that of the highest 20% grew even faster, continuing to "pull away from the pack" (Mischel et al. 2003: 5). These changes would have been more dramatic save that both low-income and, especially, middle-income households increased significantly the number of hours worked in comparison with those of higher incomes.[9]

In 1977, average after-tax income for the highest quintile was some 8 times larger than that of the lowest and 2.5 times larger than that of the middle; by 1999, the gaps had grown to 11.6 and 3.25 times larger respectively. Figures for the very rich are far more glaring. The highest 5%, with after-tax income some 14 times that of the lowest quintile in 1977, received 23 times more in 1999, and the corresponding advantage of the highest 1% went from 27 to 58 times larger. These figures exclude the effect of employer-provided health benefits and government noncash programs (housing subsidies, Medicaid/Medicare, food stamps, and the like) along with realized capital gains. Even after such corrections, however, the distance between the highest and lowest quintiles widened more than 25% over this period, and the gap opened by the very rich remains staggering. By any sensible income definition, "persistent and comparable growth of inequality" appears, "with the 1990s income inequality growth about 30% to 40% as much as in the 1980s" (Mischel et al. 2001: 69; see also Mischel et al. 2003: 70).

This inequality is unrivaled in the industrialized world. On one study, using 1996 data from the World Bank, the income of the highest fifth in Japan was some 4.3 times more than that of the lowest; in Belgium and Germany, the corresponding figures were 4.6 and 5.8; in Canada and France, the difference was 7.1; and in the United Kingdom, 9.6. Here, as mentioned, the multiple exceeds 11 (Phillips: 124). In 1997, another study concludes, United States households in

---

9. The Census Bureau's report on 2001 "suggested that the gap between rich and poor continued to grow." During that year, "the proportion of Americans living in poverty rose significantly," while the "average income for the top five percent of households rose by $1,000 . . . [and] the average declined or stayed about the same for most other income brackets" (*The New York Times*, September 25, 2002: A19). Moreover, the rate of growth in inequality also increased in 2001 after its decrease in the later 1990s (Mischel et al. 2003: 51f.).

the tenth percentile had incomes at 38% of the median, while household incomes in the ninetieth percentile were 214% of the median – a breach significantly beyond, insofar as data are available, that in any other of the twenty industrialized countries belonging to the Organization for Economic Cooperation and Development (OECD) (Mischel et al. 2003: 411). Although precision is more difficult with international comparisons, the summary result seems clear: Since the 1970s, our economy "has consistently produced the highest levels of economic inequality," and, moreover, our inequality "has shown a strong tendency to rise, even as inequality was relatively stable or declining in most of the rest of the OECD" (Mischel et al. 2003: 396).

At least to first appearances, state complicity in this disparity and, especially, in its continuing expansion are profound violations of justice as general emancipation. Maximizing the access to general emancipatory conditions equally available to all seems to demand for the less advantaged a far greater measure of available economic resources than is presently the case. The point is not complete equality of results. Some inequalities may be prescribed or permitted because, in this way, the empowerment of all is increased. Wisdom and experience counsel that everyone's welfare is greater if certain differences in responsibility and initiative occasion differing economic rewards. Moreover, political pursuit of anything approaching complete equality would so invade freedom of economic association and exchange and so heighten the consequences of political abuse that loss to the common good would be immense. But unequal access to economic benefits should stretch no further than is needed to increase creative opportunity for all and, insofar, mutuality in our life together. By this standard of justice, it is acutely difficult to see how governmental indifference to present circumstances can be justified.

As mentioned previously, confirming this judgment waits on attending to relations among the several general conditions of creativity, and some argue that our economic inequality is the price we must pay for maximizing overall the general empowerment equally enjoyed, even by the least advantaged. Without pursuing in detail the form or forms such an argument might take, we can mention some of the barriers to its success. For one, the most sophisticated attempts to assess "social health," which measure a range of factors such as child poverty, the percentage of those finishing high school, youth homicide, health-care coverage, and the like, have shown "a more or less steady decline from the high-water marks of the 1970s" (Phillips: 167; see also 344–6). Further, the complicity of economic differences with other relevant inequalities seems evident. To all appearances, the process of electing officials has, at all levels of government, been affected by recent distributional changes. Concentrated wealth in the United States has always translated into political power. As campaign expenditures have escalated, however, the sway of large donors over electoral success and thus over policy directions has been magnified, and the result is a sacrifice in substantive equality of political access.[10] A similar correlation can doubtless be drawn with inequality in public school funding – and, again, with inequity in the criminal justice system, where the rich, focused on their own security in more or less segregated communities, are often indifferent to corruption that mostly harms the poor.

In any event, a defense of our economic distribution based on its wider contribution to mutuality is bound to show why this contribution has required since the 1970s dramatically increased economic inequality and, further, how the lower 60% of citizens are served by stagnant or worsening economic conditions while the upper 40%, and especially the upper 5%, receive all of the increased economic benefits.[11] With respect to what conditions of emancipation, we may ask, has greater access for all required this expanding inequality of income? Naturally, this discussion could be pursued at length, although probably enough has been said to place the burden of proof

---

10. On the relation between formative rights to public liberties and substantive equality of political access, see Chapter 4, Section II.
11. The most frequently heard defense insists that all are served by maximizing economic freedom and thus minimizing political interference with production and distribution through the free market. Typically, however, this argument assumes a liberal ideal of community, such that the social order is properly designed to maximize the resources with which private interests may be satisfied. Whatever its merit in that context, the case requires restatement in view of justice as general creative opportunity, and how the defense could then be successful is not readily apparent. In either context, moreover, and whatever one might finally say about the importance of a free market system, there seems ample reason to call this defense disingenuous. In fact, the dynamics of our economy, especially with respect to the distribution of its benefits, are deeply affected by governmental activities. Tax policy is an obvious example. During the 1980s, changes in the federal tax code, which overall became more regressive, exacerbated the growth of inequality, although changes in the 1990s, especially the expansion of the Earned Income Tax Credit, mitigated this trend (Mishel et al. 2001: 68). The structure of state and local taxes is notoriously regressive. Even more significant, I expect, are the many ways in which governmental policies during recent decades actively assisted the owners of major corporations – from deregulation to extravagant depreciation allowances to corporate bailouts to trade policies promoting globalization. Summarily stated,

on any who would defend the current economic distribution in the United States as consistent with justice as general emancipation. Be that as it may, the intent here is to illustrate the contemporary importance of politics as a Christian vocation, and to this end I will henceforth assume that our current economic inequality is an offense to the community of love. On this assumption, politics as a Christian vocation is bound to advocate laws and policies that will increase the measure of creative opportunity equally available to all by increasing the equality of income.

Treatment of the poor is an obvious place to start. Whether supported by welfare or employed in the lowest-paying positions, up to 20% of the American people live in poverty, depending on the criteria used to mark this situation. Even by the official standard that virtually all agree is inadequate, 11.3% of the population was poor in 2000 (31.5 million people) and 11.7% in 2001 (32.9 million) (Mischel et al. 2003: 312). Since the 1970s, the poverty rate, having fallen by half over the previous 15 years, has been intransigent. Measuring 11.1% in 1973, it has been higher ever since, sometimes reaching more than 14% – in spite of productivity growth of 52% and real income per capita growth of 60% between 1973 and 2000 (Mischel et al. 2003: 312, 11). The poor have also become more deeply poor. In the 1970s, some 30% were below one-half of the poverty line; by the late 1990s, closer to 40% were in this condition (Mischel et al. 2003: 327). In 2001 dollars, the average poor family was over $1,000 poorer in 2000 than in 1973 (Mischel et al. 2003: 328). While more sophisticated standards of poverty yield higher estimates of how many are poor, the general trends are not affected (Mischel et al. 2003: 311).

No doubt, a number of forces are involved in these outcomes, but it seems clear that "the growth of inequality was the largest component adding to poverty rates over the past 30 years" (Mischel et al. 2003: 356). Since economic disparity in the United States surpasses that in any other OECD country, it is no surprise that poverty comparisons across the same countries show the rate here to be unsurpassed and

we may take for granted that the power of concentrated income and wealth will always be used to bend public policy in its direction. One sign of this, already mentioned, is the striking increase in political campaign expenditures, supported by large donors, that has followed rising economic inequality. For an extended argument that "laissez-faire is a pretense" and that "conservative rhetoric about leaving everything to the market-place was misleading," see Phillips; citations are from xiv and 93.

mobility out of poverty the most limited. (Mischel et al. 2003: 414f.). Further, the correlation in OECD countries between lesser social expenditures by the government and higher rates of poverty appears itself to be high (Mischel et al. 2003: 414, 422). Although commendation of specific programs waits on more detailed discussion, it also seems apparent that poverty in America, like income inequality, cannot be addressed without political policies directed to reversing entrenched patterns.

The tax system seems another clear focus for change. Given the maldistribution we now suffer, for instance, the federal tax cuts legislated in 2001 and 2003, heavily weighted toward the rich, in significant part through reductions in the inheritance tax and the tax on dividends, seem transparently unjust.[12] The funding of government in the several states, which relies especially on property and sales and excise taxes, is notoriously regressive, adding to whatever inequality the economy itself effects. Still, for whatever it is worth, I expect that the larger issue for public policy concerns the domination of our social order by the profit pursuits of large corporations. In the longer run, I judge, commitment to justice as general emancipation will seek policy that effects greater governance over their consequences for our common life.

If their faith indicts our economic inequality, Christians have cause to pursue the sources of general public indifference to distributional changes during recent decades. Following the course of our previous discussions, we may again ask specifically whether rival religious convictions have been effective in shaping United States policy. On my reading, both liberal and conservative ideals for community are implicated in this injustice, as I will now try to explain.

Given the liberal belief that each individual defines for herself or himself the substance of a good life, the only common measure of living better, beyond basic health and safety, is a higher "standard of living" or greater economic benefits with which to satisfy one's wants or realize one's interests. To be sure, this ideal gives no reason why an individual ought to choose ends that require greater economic resources; she or he may, for instance, prefer a modest life, emphasizing appreciation of the natural world or participation in one or more

---

12. Apropos of the tax on dividends, 47.7% of all stocks in 1998 were owned by the top 1% of all households; the bottom 80% owned 4.1% (Mischel et al. 2003: 9).

associations. It remains, however, that larger social structures should serve private ends, in the sense that the larger community is commonly taken to be instrumental. Liberals are, therefore, easily led to see this service as greater or less in terms of the instrumental resources economic benefits provide, from which it follows that economic goals and processes should be supreme within the social order and public purpose. Subject to whatever constraints constitutional duties and supposed rules of fairness assign, the general purpose of society becomes maximal production and distribution of goods and services that can be used for diverse private interests. The power of this ideal in American life, at least since the Civil War, provides, I judge, the religious background for our evolution into what is called summarily a "consumer society."

Moreover, the supremacy of economic goals during this period has reinforced itself and, thereby, the liberal ideal. Economic advance has made massive contributions to emancipation. But its benefits have also insidiously persuaded Americans, in part through the self-promotion of economic institutions, that quality of life is principally defined by the extent to which one enjoys such benefits. Mutuality, at least in the larger social order, is not affirmed for its own sake but, rather, as a form of exchange and, thereby, economic increase, and each individual or household is led to focus on the economic resources it commands. As one consequence, politics is seen to be and thus tends to become another arena for economic conflict and bargaining. Barring a threat to basic health and safety, the main concern of most citizens is the effect of governmental policy on their own economic standing, and, roughly summarized, assurance that it will not seriously deteriorate is a precondition for attention to other values.

Insofar as the liberal view reduces politics to this kind of bargaining, the outcome principally depends on the relative power differing participants can direct to satisfying their private interests. Absent other considerations, the more economically advantaged will marshal greater political power and, accordingly, have greater control over the results, whereby their advantage is reinforced. Something like this has occurred in United States politics in the past thirty years. I have in mind especially the measure in which a political ideology of limited national government and reliance on the free market system has been effective. This does not deny that those economically advantaged have also achieved governmental interventions beneficial to their position, especially with respect to tax and corporate policy. The use of superior power need not always be consistent with the ideology that serves it. But the general homage paid to political nonintervention has, among other things, militated against policies designed to effect greater assistance to the poor or redistribution of income and wealth. The distribution of economic benefits is insofar left more or less entirely to the working of the market system itself, where advantage typically leads to greater advantage, and economic inequality expands.

To be sure, other commitments might counter the outcomes of a political process prone to conflict and bargaining among economic interests. Welfare liberals, for instance, might advocate a basic economic level for all, in a sense that requires state revision of the distribution that otherwise occurs. But these advocates in effect spite themselves by sharing with libertarian liberals an economic measure of the good life. Seen through that measure, a decrease in one's standard of living is a sacrifice in happiness, and this counsels the rich to weigh their power against policies that reduce their share. In truth, moreover, a principle of greater economic equality cannot be derived from the aim at maximal satisfaction of one's own private interests, so that, finally, the political purposes of welfare liberals are inconsistent with the view of happiness they commend. Redistribution will, therefore, always be resisted just insofar as an economic measure of human flourishing is effective among those who have more.

Indeed, no one, rich or poor, who applies this measure is encouraged to make inequality itself an issue, because what matters for each individual or household is not what others have but, rather, its own level of economic rewards. Whatever force should be granted to sentiments of envy, the politically more consequential comparison for those among the less advantaged is not to the more advantaged but, rather, to their own previous situation. Has there been increase? For this reason, the important political question concerns economic growth in which all participate, however uneven the shares. A rising tide that raises all ships has been largely sufficient to prevent discord over economic distribution just because the liberal ideal has been so pervasively affirmed.

For all that, however, political strife has emerged when a widening gap occurs while income decreases in the middle level and below. The populist movements of the later nineteenth century and the Great

Depression of the 1930s exemplify this set of circumstances. As noted, expanding disparity in the 1980s and 1990s left the real income of most Americans at best stagnant. So why, notwithstanding the limits of liberal perspectives, has there been no significant political challenge to a tide that has failed to reach so many harbors?

In large part, I believe, this absence betrays the national appearance in strength of the conservative communal ideal. During recent decades, it has deflected attention from inequalities in the social order toward issues of personal morality. After threats to inherited norms of private virtue that occurred or were perceived to occur during the volatile events of the 1960s, this ideal gained in political importance. Issues of abortion, homosexuality, affirmative action, family responsibility, family control of education, and the like increasingly influenced political alignments. Focus on private virtue cut across various income levels and, especially, was widely shared by members of the broad middle class with persons among the most advantaged, thereby undermining an alliance based on common economic interest that middle-class and lower-class Americans might have forged against the wealthy.

In contrast to their more traditional focus on state and local politics, I previously suggested, conservatives emerged to seek national effect because, as they saw things, the federal government, including the Supreme Court, had become increasingly hostile to the freedom with which state and local governments might work in support of "traditional values." The school prayer and *Roe v. Wade* decisions were two illustrations of the Court's complicity. Conservatives thus came to share with partisans of unfettered markets an active distrust of the federal government (see Lowi: chap. 5). Whatever its internal disagreements, this coalition has shaped national politics ever since. If the liberal ideal alone tends to suppress concern over maldistribution, given only that everyone benefits somewhat from economic growth, protest has been the more absent from public view because even the agenda of welfare liberals has been thrown on the defensive. Hence the virtual silence on this issue in both major political parties.

This summary of recent American politics obviously includes many particular judgments with which other interpretations may disagree. Insofar as it has merit, however, it underscores that liberal and conservative ideals for community and, in this sense, religious convictions have been consequential in the dynamics of public life leading to our current economic inequality. It then follows that here, too, Christians have reason to find religious choices at stake in future democratic decisions. Seeking a major reversal of the distributional march we have taken, politics as a Christian vocation involves an explicit or implicit call for radical change in the religious background of our public life.

IV CONCLUSION

A transformed religious background is imperative far beyond the issue of economic inequality. In presenting this judgment, I will do no more than assert it, because this work does not aim to reach a particular set of political purposes. But I do wish to say that change in the effective communal ideal is broadly important for the same principal reasons that escalating economic inequality has been largely ignored. I have in mind the power in our political community exercised by liberal and conservative religious convictions.

As it has for generations, the liberal ideal continues to persuade most Americans most of the time that our national purpose, subject to constitutional constraints and some or other rules of fairness, should maximize economic provision and growth because the larger community is properly designed to facilitate maximal satisfaction of private interests. So long as this ideal has a controlling effect on the federal government, there will be no adequate address to issues that include, among others, poverty, substantive political equality, the funding of public services, and the capacity of economic institutions to help perpetuate that ideal itself. Those persuaded by the conservative ideal rightly reject the liberal equation of human good with want-satisfaction and expose some of its debasing effects on human character and human relationships. But the focus on private virtue prevents political attention to most inequities in general emancipation. Accordingly, conservative political purposes do not challenge most social structural conditions of human debasement or the injustice of permitting or supporting them. As a consequence, even private virtue can be defined in narrow ways inconsistent with the emancipation of all, for instance, in some characterizations of sexual responsibility or of proper cultural taste and expression.

The promise of American democracy, according to Thomas Jefferson, is "public happiness" (Jefferson: 65), providing and promoting a community through which "we the people" flourish. Its achievement, so far as I can see, now waits on pervasive public commitment to mutuality as the principal worldly source and inclusive worldly end of each individual's creativity. Directed by that ideal, the economic order becomes subservient to association for its own sake, proper forms of diversity are defined in terms of mutual enrichment, and responsibilities of the state are specified in relation to maximizing the measure in which all are empowered. Only the ideal of maximal mutuality, I believe, deserves our inclusive loyalty because only the God whom Christians experience through Jesus Christ can authorize any purpose at all. Human life has worth only because it is embraced and cherished forever by that God.

As they pursue their democratic vocation, Christians naturally have every reason to make common cause on particular issues with fellow citizens who reach similar positions based on divergent terms of assessment. To welcome them as allies is simply to honor the sovereignty of every citizen over her or his assessment of every political claim. But if we require transformation of the dominant communal ideal or ideals, then politics as a Christian vocation includes more than advocacy of particular political purposes. Although fitting occasions and formulations require sensitivity to context, Christians are called to public criticism of the competing religious convictions implicated in political debates or decisions and to public assertion and defense of the community of love. A radical change in the religious background of our life together will not occur without explicit disclosure of the religious decisions at stake and explicit witness to the God Christians re-present as all-embracing love.

Even here, however, Christians will misconstrue their vocation if they think that common cause can include only other Christians. The experience of Jesus Christians confess re-presents the divine purpose of which all humans are aware and for which they are called to decide in every moment of their lives. This is why Christian faith can be assessed in a full and free political discourse. Christians, therefore, should readily affirm that their God may also be re-presented in other religions or other symbols and concepts expressing the ultimate terms of political assessment, even if the only God that could be truly re-presented elsewhere is the God revealed through Jesus

Christ. Wherever or insofar as they find others committed to the same ultimate ground of worth, Christians are in all essentials at one with their fellow citizens and are called by their common God to make their common religious claim. Thereby, the point of religious freedom will be exemplified, and, if Christian faith can indeed be redeemed by the way of reason, democracy as "the last, best hope of earth" will be vindicated.

Appendix

On the Humanistic Commitment

Government by the people, this work has argued, is politics through full and free discourse. Democracy, therefore, presupposes the humanistic commitment. It affirms that reason, "universal and yet individual to each," is the "ultimate judge ... to which all authority must bow" (Whitehead 1961: 162) – or that reasons authorized finally by common human experience are alone sufficient to validate any understanding that can be validated. Specifically, popular sovereignty depends on the possibility of assessing by argument the validity of religious claims and thus claims for ultimate terms of political assessment. But commitment to the way of reason, as I have called it, is today widely rejected, both by religious adherents and by those who purport to hold no such conviction at all. Throughout the extended diversity of our political community, one might even say, the exclusion of religious convictions from validation and invalidation through discourse is the one opinion about religion on which there is near consensus.

A similar view dominates academic discussion. Chapter 2 reviewed alternative accounts of a democratic constitution and noted especially those for which justice is independent of any conception of the comprehensive good. Typically, theories pursue that separation in order to affirm religious freedom notwithstanding their assumption that religious differences cannot themselves be adjudicated in public discourse. Quite apart from discussions of democracy, moreover, many thinkers hold that rationality is misconceived when taken to be the arbiter of claims for universal principles of belief or practice. This view, sometimes associated with "postmodern" thought, is often said to follow from modern historical consciousness. The very notion of common human experience is, in effect, denied and, with it, the supposition that religious claims define a rational order of reflection.

Once contested, the way of reason itself is especially difficult to assess in a clear and convincing manner. The focus of our thinking then becomes the proper character of our thinking insofar as we seek to validate and invalidate our understandings or beliefs. When we turn critical thought on itself in this way, we are especially susceptible to taking for granted something we need to put under examination, thereby begging the question. Nonetheless, no critical accounting of our life together can be complete without clarification of whether and, if so, how critical thought can address our most fundamental differences. For any who might have an interest in this issue, this appendix offers a summary defense of the humanistic commitment and its implications with respect to the religious question.

Given the contemporary philosophical discussion, no attempt to redeem the way of reason can be fully adequate absent sustained engagement with alternative ways in which the critique of reason has been advanced. But that course would extend this appendix into another work. In lieu of it, I will argue summarily that the way of reason should be affirmed because critically asking about it already implies commitment to it. This question, I will try to show, is unlike most others because it is self-answering.

I speak of a question as self-answering when only one possible answer is self-consistent, so that any other response one might give is senseless. Hence, fully to understand the question is already to have all one needs to determine its valid answer because invalid answers finally defeat or refute themselves. Most questions we ask and answer about the world or ourselves are not of this kind. To be sure, most may have only one true answer, but false answers are not simply senseless. For instance, if we seek the approximate circumference of the earth or ask which president of the United States was the most eloquent, the true answers may be "25,000 miles" and "Abraham Lincoln," respectively. Still, a belief that someone who circles the globe travels 10,000 miles or that Calvin Coolidge was unrivaled as a rhetorician is not mere nonsense; that is, one cannot determine simply by careful analysis of these affirmations that they refute themselves. Consider, in contrast, the question "Do I exist?" As many have held, following Descartes' famous argument, this question is self-answering. A negative answer defeats itself because asking the question implies a simultaneous affirmation of one's own existence. In a similar way, I will now argue, the question "Is it true that understandings can be validated only through reasons authorized finally by common human experience?" has only one self-consistent answer.[1]

Let us note first that critical address to this question depends on the valid answer. Whether the humanistic commitment is or is not credible, our thinking here seeks to validate an answer, and we need to know whether *this* validation will or will not be by argument. Further reflection will confirm that we can critically answer this question by argument only if, in fact, the commitment is credible. I recognize that some have sought to argue against the way of reason, so that, in effect, reason is said to critique itself or set its own limits with respect to validation. So far as I can see, however, no such argument could be successful. A critique of reason in this sense requires some concept of what lies beyond the limits it sets; a limit with nothing beyond is not a limit. But argument cannot successfully defend a concept of nonrational validation; were that to be achieved, anything validated in the latter way would, in truth, be redeemed by argument.

Aquinas, at least on one reading of him, can be said to argue for the following: Understandings of God's character can be validated only by appeal to God's special revelation through Jesus. Were any argument for this conclusion sound, however, understandings validated in the manner prescribed would, in truth, be established by the way of reason. Hence, if knowing the character of God requires appeal beyond the limits of reason, this denial of the humanistic commitment also transcends those limits. On some postmodern accounts, as mentioned previously, our capacities for rational validation are said to be circumscribed by our historicity, that is, our specific cultural inheritance or historical location. The point here, then, is simply this: If it denies the humanistic commitment, no such view can be established by argument, because the account of rational validation asserted cannot be circumscribed by any specific location. A critique of universal reason can itself be a reasoned critique only if validation of its conclusions transcends the limits it sets to validation by reason.

---

1. The self-refutation explicated here is a pragmatic self-contradiction; that is, every subject who affirms the understanding in question simultaneously affirms its contradictory. I have discussed the relation between pragmatic and conceptual forms of self-contradiction in Gamwell 1990: chap. 4.

Here too, then, the way of reason can be denied only if that denial cannot itself be redeemed by that way.

In sum, we can validate by argument the right answer to our question only if that answer is positive, and, if that answer is negative, we cannot successfully argue for it. If some understandings of reality and ourselves can be validated without appeal to reason and common human experience, the statement of this fact must express one of those understandings. Let us reformulate the point as follows: In asking about the humanistic commitment, we cannot validate an answer without presupposing that answer. Arrival at this outcome, some may now say, reveals that the question cannot be answered without begging it; validation of either answer involves a vicious circle. Thus, each of us must simply choose which course to take. As it happens, something like this conclusion has been asserted by some Christian thinkers. On their account, commitment to the way of reason is itself an alternative "faith," meaning that it cannot impartially validate itself, and Christians have no cause to submit their faith in God to rational assessment. Indeed, doing so would be, in effect, religious conversion.

But this line of thought is fallacious. If the humanistic commitment is, in truth, an alternative faith in the sense asserted, then, in truth, religious claims cannot be validated or invalidated by argument, because all validation assumes a prior decision for some particular faith. Hence, one could not sensibly decide for or convert to the way of reason. Moreover, the line of thought offered reaches its conclusion as an implication of our question and thus asserts, in effect, that only a negative answer is sensible. Hence, validation of the negative answer can itself occur by argument and does *not* depend on a faith simply chosen, and this contradicts the premise that neither answer can be validated without a vicious circle. In truth, the humanistic commitment is not itself a faith, in the sense that it is or involves a conviction about the ultimate ground of worth and the inclusive orientation proper to human life, because, in itself, affirmation of the way of reason says nothing about what understanding of ultimate worth can be validated. This is not to deny that the humanistic commitment is, in another sense, a faith, namely, as an aspect of every primal decision for a self-understanding, whatever its content may otherwise be. Every such decision implies a claim for its own authenticity and, if the way of reason can be redeemed, thereby implicitly claims validity for an understanding of human existence in relation to its ultimate ground that discourse can validate. In this sense, to live in the distinctively human way is inescapably to live with the faith that the ultimate worth of life is rational.

Seeing that our question cannot imply a negative answer suggests another possibility: The only sensible answer is positive. I will commend this conclusion by first stating the grounds for it and then seeking to defend them. The valid answer, we have said, cannot be validated without presupposing it, because it defines what counts as validation. But the positive and negative answers differ in this: To show that the humanistic commitment is not credible, we must not only assume this very conclusion but *also* presuppose to the contrary. The way of reason is presupposed by both answers; hence, a negative answer contradicts itself, and the only sensible answer is positive.

We are bound to this conclusion because, in asking the question, we presuppose that one of the two answers is valid and the other invalid. This means that neither answer can be validated simply by being a possible answer; validation requires appeal to considerations other than the mere fact that the answer is given. A negative answer, however, has nothing to which it can appeal except the assertion of it. Naturally, one might appeal to the supposed authority of some institutional or cultural inheritance or religious tradition. But this does not change the outcome because claims for this authority are merely asserted, supposedly validated by the fact that they are made. To the contrary, then, asking whether the humanistic commitment is credible presupposes that *reasons* can be presented through which one answer or the other is validated, that is, presupposes validation by argument. Since we can argue for the right answer only if that answer is positive, asking the question and, therefore, giving either answer presuppose the way of reason. Some may object that a positive answer also has nothing to which it might appeal except its own assertion. But they are mistaken. The humanistic commitment is validated by the argument that it alone is the coherent alternative, its denial being self-defeating because both answers affirm validation by the giving of reasons. Hence, the way of reason, once it is entertained, cannot be consistently refused. Asking about it commits us to it.

Assuming that this conclusion is sound, we may clarify further the distinctively religious question: What is the ultimate ground of worth and what inclusive purpose for human life does it authorize? I have proposed taking the central terms of this question in extended senses, whereby "ultimate ground of worth" designates whatever grounds ultimate terms for political assessment, and some or other inclusive purpose is asserted even if one holds that there is no single purpose for all human life (see Chapter 2, Section III). To be sure, the question itself might be dismissed as a pseudoquestion, its extended meaning notwithstanding. One might hold that it has no valid answer. So far as I can see, this can only mean that there are no valid terms for moral or political assessment at all, and all moral and political claims are finally mere expressions of subjective preference or approval, as has often been asserted in Western thought. I further believe that this understanding of human life is, in effect, simply another answer to the religious question. But I will not pause here to defend that accounting. For present purposes, I will take for granted that the religious question is a sensible one or has a valid answer. To be sure, one might concede this assumption and still deny that religious convictions can be validated and invalidated. The valid answer, one might hold, is unknowable. But this view is not tenable because the question asks about ultimate terms for moral and political assessment. As discussed in Chapter 3, we cannot have unknowable moral obligations. Ignorance of what we ought to do means that we cannot do it because we ought to do so (see Chapter 3, Section III).

Given commitment to the way of reason, we can now recognize that the religious question must also be self-answering; only one answer can be sensible. This, too, is because every answer purports to designate the ultimate ground of worth. Were the question not self-answering, it would be impossible to assess religious convictions by the way of reason, since there can be no more fundamental terms of evaluation to which we might appeal to validate and invalidate proposed understandings of the inclusive purpose. Hence, false religious convictions – or, better, religious convictions insofar as they misrepresent the ultimate ground of worth and human purpose – must be, as with any self-answering question, self-defeating or self-refuting.

In a manner similar to asking about one's own existence, then, asking about the ultimate ground of worth implies a simultaneous affirmation of or belief in the valid answer. To be sure, this answer is far less readily apparent than a belief in one's own existence. Hence, calling the religious question self-answering does not entail that assessment of religious claims is a simple process or that agreement on the outcome is easily reached. To the contrary, reasoning about the most fundamental question of human life has its correspondingly profound difficulties (see Chapter 3, Section I). Moreover, calling false answers self-refuting does not deny that the valid answer may be expressed or symbolized in dramatically different ways. If the Christian religion is true, for instance, this does not necessarily mean that Buddhism or Islam or Judaism is false. Because each expresses its religious understanding in a complex system of concepts and symbols, including symbolic practices, it may be that differing systems in fact express the same substantive belief. The point is solely that validity is here assessed by whether the substantive understanding for which validity is claimed is the one implied by asking the question.

Allowing that every moment of human life involves an affirmation of one's own worth, just as every moment of self-consciousness affirms one's own existence, we may conclude that Christian faith is valid at least in this respect: Every human always includes at the deepest level of awareness a true belief about the ultimate ground of worth. Whether this belief is truly re-presented by the Christian understanding of God is another question. But if human life were not essentially marked by awareness of what makes it ultimately worth living, the religious question would not be self-answering, and no understanding of ourselves in relation to the inclusive purpose could be redeemed. Critical reflection on re-presentations of ultimate worth is, some might say, the attempt to reach by argument something about ourselves that, at the deepest level of consciousness, we already know. With Whitehead, this true belief is the "ultimate judge, universal and yet individual to each," and its presence in common human experience is what authorizes the reasons through which religious convictions are validated or invalidated. That misinterpretations are convicted by this judge is, moreover, the reflection in critical thought of the elemental fact of our existence: One cannot really decide for a false interpretation of human existence, in the sense that it defines one's primal self-understanding, without self-conviction. We live with integrity or authenticity only by embracing our abiding awareness of our ultimate condition – and, if Christian faith is indeed true, the God of all-embracing love.

Works Cited

Anselm, St. 1962. *St. Anselm: Basic Writings*, second edition, translated by S. N. Deane. LaSalle, IL: Open Court.

Apel, Karl-Otto. 1973. "Types of Rationality Today." In *Rationality Today*, edited by Theodore Gereats. Ottowa: University Press, pp. 307–40.

Aquinas, St. Thomas. 1973. *Basic Writings of St. Thomas Aquinas: Volume One: God and the Order of Creation*, edited by Anton C. Pegis. Indianapolis: Hackett Publishing. All citations from *Summa Theologicae, Part I* are from this publication.

1975a. *Summa Contra Gentiles, Book Three, Part I*, translated by Vernon J. Bourke. Notre Dame, IN: University of Notre Dame Press.

1975b. *Summa Contra Gentiles, Book Three, Part II*, translated by Vernon J. Bourke. Notre Dame, IN: University of Notre Dame Press.

1988. *On Law, Morality, and Politics*, edited by William P. Baumgarth and Richard J. Regan, S.J. Indianapolis: Hackett Publishing Company. All citations from *Summa Theologicae, Part II* and from *On Kingship* are from this volume.

Audi, Robert. 1997. "Liberal Democracy and the Place of Religion in Politics." In Robert Audi and Nicholas Wolterstorff, *Religion in the Public Square*. Lanham, MD: Rowan and Littlefield, pp. 1–66.

Augustine, St. 1984. *City of God*, translated by Henry Bettenson. New York: Penguin Books.

1993. *On Free Choice of the Will*, translated by Thomas Williams. Indanapolis: Hackett Publishing Company.

Barry, Brian. 1995. *Justice as Impartiality*. Oxford: Clarendon Press.

Beer, Samuel H. 1993. *To Make a Nation: The Rediscovery of American Federalism.* Cambridge, MA: Harvard University Press.

Buttrick, George A. 1951. "Exposition: The Gospel According to St. Matthew." In *The Interpreter's Bible,* Volume VII. New York: Abingdon Press, pp. 250–625.

Dahl, Robert A. 2001. *How Democratic Is the American Constitution?* New York: Columbia University Press.

Deane, Herbert A. 1963. *The Political and Social Ideas of St. Augustine.* New York: Columbia University Press.

Dewey, John. 1963. *Liberalism and Social Action.* New York: Capricon Books.

Dillenberger, John and Welch, Claude. 1954. *Protestant Christianity: Interpreted Through Its Development.* New York: Charles Scribner's Sons.

Dryzek, John S. 2000. *Deliberative Democracy and Beyond: Liberals, Critics, Contestations.* New York: Oxford University Press.

Dworkin, Ronald. 1996. *Freedom's Law: The Moral Reading of the American Constitution.* Cambridge, MA: Harvard University Press.

Furnish, Victor P. In press. "Uncommon Love and the Common Good: Christians as Citizens in the Letters of Paul." In *Theology and the Common Good,* edited by Dennis McCann and Patrick D. Miller. New York: T&T Clark.

Galston, William A. 2002. *Liberal Puluralism: The Implications of Value Pluralism for Political Theory and Practice.* New York: Cambridge University Press.

Gamwell, Franklin I. 1990. *The Divine Good: Modern Moral Theory and the Necessity of God.* San Francisco: HarperCollins.

1995. *The Meaning of Religious Freedom: Modern Politics and the Democratic Resolution.* Albany: State University of New York Press.

2000. *Democracy on Purpose: Justice and the Reality of God.* Washington, DC: Georgetown University Press.

2001. "Speaking of God after Aquinas." *The Journal of Religion* 81: 185–210.

2003. "The Moral Ground of Cosmopolitan Democracy." *The Journal of Religion* 83: 562–84.

Grant, Robert M. 1977. *Early Christianity and Society.* San Francisco: Harper & Row.

Habermas, Jürgen. 1990. *Moral Consciousness and Communicative Action*, translated by Christian Lenhardt and Shierry Weber Nicholson. Cambridge, MA: MIT Press.

1996. *Between Facts and Norms: Contributions to a Discourse Theory of Law and Democracy*, translated by William Rehg. Cambridge, MA: MIT Press.

Hadot, Pierre. 1995. *Philosophy as a Way of Life*, edited by Arnold I. Davidson, translated by Michael Chase. Cambridge, MA: Blackwell.

Hartshorne, Charles. 1967. *A Natural Theology for Our Time*. LaSalle, IL: Open Court.

1970. *Creative Synthesis and Philosophic Method*. LaSalle, IL: Open Court.

Hollenbach, David, S.J. 2002. *The Common Good and Christian Ethics*. New York: Cambridge University Press.

Jefferson, Thomas. 1999. *Jefferson: Political Writings*, edited by Joyce Appleby and Terence Ball. New York: Cambridge University Press.

Knox, John. 1961. *The Ethic of Jesus in the Teaching of the Church*. New York: Abingdon Press.

Larmore, Charles. 1996. *The Morals of Modernity*. New York: Cambridge University Press.

Lemann, Nicholas. 1995. "Taking Affirmative Action Apart." *New York Times Magazine* (June 11), 36–41, 52–4, 62, 66.

Lowi, Theodore J. 1995. *The End of the Republican Era*. Norman, OK: University of Oklahoma Press.

Marxsen, Willi. 1993. *New Testament Foundations for Christian Ethics*. Minneapolis: Fortress Press.

Mead, Sidney E. 1963. *The Lively Experiment: The Shaping of Christianity in America*. New York: Harper & Row.

Meeks, Wayne A. 1986. *The Moral World of the First Christians*. Philadelphia: Westminster Press.

Miller, Perry. 1956. *Errand into the Wilderness*. Cambridge, MA: Belknap Press of Harvard University Press.

Mischel, Lawrence, Bernstein, Jared, and Boushey, Heather. 2003. *The State of Working America, 2002/2003*. Ithaca, NY: Cornell University Press.

Mishel, Lawrence, Bernstein, Jared, and Schmitt, John. 2001. *The State of Working America, 2000/2001*. Ithaca, NY: Cornell University Press.

Murray, John Courtney, S.J. 1960. *We Hold These Truths: Catholic Reflections on the American Proposition*. Kansas City, MO: Sheed and Ward.

Niebuhr, Reinhold. 1941–3. *The Nature and Destiny of Man*, 2 volumes. New York: Charles Scribner's Sons.

1944. *The Children of Light and the Children of Darkness: A Vindication of Democracy and a Critique of Its Traditional Defense*. New York: Charles Scribner's Sons.

Ogden, Schubert M. 1966. *The Reality of God and Other Essays*. New York: Harper & Row.

1982. *The Point of Christology*. San Francisco: Harper & Row.

1992. *Is There Only One True Religion or Are There Many?* Dallas: Southern Methodist University Press.

Perry, Michael J. 1997. *Religion in Politics: Constitutional and Moral Perspectives*. New York: Oxford University Press.

Phillips, Kevin. 2002. *Wealth and Democracy: A Political History of the American Rich*. New York: Broadway Books.

Randall, John Herman, Jr. 1960. *Aristotle*. New York: Columbia University Press.

Rauschenbusch, Walter. 1945. *A Theology for the Social Gospel*. New York: Abingdon Press.

Rawls, John. 1971. *A Theory of Justice*. Cambridge, MA: Harvard University Press.

1996. *Political Liberalism*. New York: Columbia University Press.

Schleiermacher, Friedrich. 1989. *The Christian Faith*, edited by H. R. MacIntosh and J. S. Stewart. Edinburgh: T&T Clark.

Tillich, Paul. 1951. *Systematic Theology*, Volume I. Chicago: University of Chicago Press.

Urmson, J. O. 1988. *Aristotle's Ethics*. Oxford: Basil Blackwell.

Whitehead, Alfred North. 1938. *Modes of Thought*. New York: Macmillan Company.

1941. "Immortality." In *The Philosophy of Alfred North Whitehead*, edited by Paul A. Schilpp. Evanston, IL: Northwestern University Press, 682–700.

1958. *The Function of Reason*. Boston: Beacon Press.

1961. *Adventures of Ideas*. New York: Free Press.

1978. *Process and Reality*, corrected edition, edited by David Ray Griffin and Donald W. Sherburne. New York: Free Press.

Wolin, Sheldon S. 1960. *Politics and Vision: Continuity and Innovation in Western Political Thought*. Boston: Little, Brown and Company.

Index